Pro Tools HD: Advanced Techniques and Workflows

Learn how to make the most of Pro Tools HD 11

Edouard Camou

PUBLISHING

BIRMINGHAM - MUMBAI

Pro Tools HD: Advanced Techniques and Workflows

First published: October 2013

Production Reference: 1181013

Published by Packt Publishing Ltd.
Livery Place
35 Livery Street
Birmingham B3 2PB, UK.

ISBN 978-1-84969-816-0

www.packtpub.com

Cover Image by Edouard Camou (ed@sinewavz.com)

Credits

Author
Edouard Camou

Reviewers
Roey Izhaki

Marco Sonzini

Acquisition Editors
Sam Birch

Mary Nadar

Commissioning Editor
Meeta Rajani

Technical Editors
Amit Ramadas

Amit Shetty

Copy Editors
Brandt D'Mello

Gladson Monteiro

Adithi Shetty

Kirti Pai

Project Coordinator
Akash Poojary

Proofreader
Stephen Swaney

Indexers
Monica Ajmera Mehta

Rekha Nair

Graphics
Sheetal Aute

Production Coordinator
Conidon Miranda

Cover Work
Conidon Miranda

About the Author

Edouard Camou is a French sound engineer and the founder of the Sinewavz sound services in London. He has many years' experience in the studio and the live music industry, supported by a Recording Arts degree (with a first class) and an Avid Pro Tools certification. He studied and worked at SAE for a while and then redesigned and upgraded Musicland Studios in London, which now has two live rooms and a bigger control room to focus on band recording, album mixing and mastering. Edouard has been involved on many different projects for artists, labels, post-production companies, video games, acoustics, and live venues. He also mastered a single that became a 2012 favorite on national UK radio.

About the Reviewers

Roey Izhaki is the author of *Mixing Audio*. He has been involved with mixing since the early 90s. He is an academic lecturer in the field of audio engineering and gives mixing seminars across Europe at various schools and exhibitions. He is currently lecturing at the Audio Engineering department at SAE Institute, London.

Marco Sonzini, 28, is an Italian-born audio engineer and a Pro Tools operator. He approached the music world at age 7, studying classical guitar at Conservatorio Nicolini in Piacenza throughout middle school and high school. He graduated with a degree in Science and Technology of Music Communication at the University of Milan, then he moved to Los Angeles, completing his degree with honors in the Audio Engineering program at the Los Angeles Recording School, where he also became a Pro Tools 210M and 210P Certified Operator.

www.PacktPub.com

Support files, eBooks, discount offers and more

You might want to visit www.PacktPub.com for support files and downloads related to your book.

Did you know that Packt offers eBook versions of every book published, with PDF and ePub files available? You can upgrade to the eBook version at www.PacktPub.com and as a print book customer, you are entitled to a discount on the eBook copy. Get in touch with us at service@packtpub.com for more details.

At www.PacktPub.com, you can also read a collection of free technical articles, sign up for a range of free newsletters and receive exclusive discounts and offers on Packt books and eBooks.

http://PacktLib.PacktPub.com

Do you need instant solutions to your IT questions? PacktLib is Packt's online digital book library. Here, you can access, read and search across Packt's entire library of books.

Why Subscribe?

- Fully searchable across every book published by Packt
- Copy and paste, print and bookmark content
- On demand and accessible via web browser

Free Access for Packt account holders

If you have an account with Packt at www.PacktPub.com, you can use this to access PacktLib today and view nine entirely free books. Simply use your login credentials for immediate access.

Table of Contents

Preface

Pro Tools is a very powerful software full of functionalities. This book is designed as a comprehensive guide for advanced user techniques to improve workflow and creative use of the software.

What this book covers

Chapter 1, *System Optimization*, helps you understand the technology behind Pro Tools to get the best out of it.

Chapter 2, *Editing Techniques*, discusses the advanced use of editing tools, Beat Detective, and Elastic Audio to improve and manipulate audio.

Chapter 3, *Advanced Mixing*, helps you integrate analog equipment into your mix and learn how to use internal routing and automations to increase creative output.

Chapter 4, *Importing and Exporting Options*, highlights good file management practices to import, export, recover, and also help the workflow of our mix.

What you need for this book

To use the techniques described in this book, you will need a Pro Tools HD Accel, HDX, or HD Native system, or a Pro Tools 10 license with Complete Production Toolkit. Basic Pro Tools knowledge is also recommended.

Who this book is for

This book is for any Pro Tools user wishing to get more out of the software. It not only relates to advanced Pro Tools tools and techniques, but is also accessible through the use of many examples and a step-by-step approach where we link and discuss the software features for real-world use.

Conventions

In this book, you will find a number of styles of text that distinguish between different kinds of information. Here are some examples of these styles, and an explanation of their meaning.

Code words in text are shown as follows: "Create a new track name `Recording` and select the same input number as the one used for the insert."

New terms and **important words** are shown in bold. Words that you see on the screen, in menus or dialog boxes for example, appear in the text like this: "Navigate to **Preferences | Display | Color Coding**."

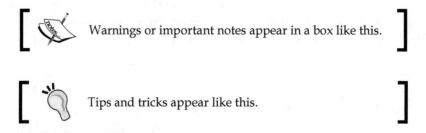

Reader feedback

Feedback from our readers is always welcome. Let us know what you think about this book—what you liked or may have disliked. Reader feedback is important for us to develop titles that you really get the most out of.

To send us general feedback, simply send an e-mail to `feedback@packtpub.com`, and mention the book title via the subject of your message.

If there is a topic that you have expertise in and you are interested in either writing or contributing to a book, see our author guide on `www.packtpub.com/authors`.

Customer support

Now that you are the proud owner of a Packt book, we have a number of things to help you to get the most from your purchase.

Downloading the color images of this book

We also provide you a PDF file that has color images of the screenshots/diagrams used in this book. The color images will help you better understand the changes in the output. You can download this file from `http://www.packtpub.com/sites/default/files/downloads/8160OT_Graphics.pdf`.

Errata

Although we have taken every care to ensure the accuracy of our content, mistakes do happen. If you find a mistake in one of our books—maybe a mistake in the text or the code—we would be grateful if you would report this to us. By doing so, you can save other readers from frustration and help us improve subsequent versions of this book. If you find any errata, please report them by visiting `http://www.packtpub.com/submit-errata`, selecting your book, clicking on the **errata submission form** link, and entering the details of your errata. Once your errata are verified, your submission will be accepted and the errata will be uploaded on our website, or added to any list of existing errata, under the Errata section of that title. Any existing errata can be viewed by selecting your title from `http://www.packtpub.com/support`.

Piracy

Piracy of copyright material on the Internet is an ongoing problem across all media. At Packt, we take the protection of our copyright and licenses very seriously. If you come across any illegal copies of our works, in any form, on the Internet, please provide us with the location address or website name immediately so that we can pursue a remedy.

Please contact us at `copyright@packtpub.com` with a link to the suspected pirated material.

We appreciate your help in protecting our authors, and our ability to bring you valuable content.

Questions

You can contact us at `questions@packtpub.com` if you are having a problem with any aspect of the book, and we will do our best to address it.

1
System Optimization

In this chapter, we will discuss the various Pro Tools hardware and software setups for mixing and recording as well as their architecture and possible limits. We will also look at some interesting tips to improve our MIDI workflow.

The Pro Tools range

Pro Tools is currently undergoing a transition period for its professional solutions. The legacy hardware HD Accel is now being replaced by HDX, allowing users to choose between different technologies and setups. Simultaneously, the software has been updated to versions 10 and 11, two major updates that now coexist with three types of technologies. In this book we will focus on the latest Pro Tools HD range compared to the legacy HD Accel.

- HD Accel
- HDX
- HD Native
- Pro Tools HD 10
- Pro Tools 10 (formerly LE) with the full production toolkit (CPTK)
- Pro Tools HD 11

Next, we will look at the different possible hardware and software options and discuss how choosing one or the other could affect your workflow. Since we can combine software and hardware in different ways, it is important to compare their strengths and understand their limitations.

Hardware solutions

Avid currently sells HDX and **HD Native** solutions but still supports the legacy Accel range. This new range came along with a brand new set of interfaces, replacing the legacy Accel range but still supporting 192 and 96 "blue" interfaces that we will not discuss here. However, it is worth mentioning that they really increased the sound quality of their AD and DA convertors, bringing the Avid HD range to sit among the best sounding interfaces in the market. Let's now have a look at the Avid range of DSP cards.

Pro Tools HD Accel

The audio industry flagship for many years, Pro Tools HD Accel is a DSP-based system using **Time Division Multiplexing (TDM)** coding. It became very expensive because the user would need to purchase many additional cards to achieve a comfortable amount of processing power. You can have up to seven cards per computer for an HD7. Even if it is now technologically unjustified, its quality and studio presence are still current, and since you can still use it with PT10 (PT11 does not support it anymore), we should discuss it.

Pro Tools HD Accel operates at 24-bit for TDM plugin processing with a 48-bit, fixed-point summing engine. Its DSP chips can run specially coded TDM plugins, but its delay compensation engine is limited to a maximum of 4095 samples. **Real Time Audio Suite (RTAS)** can also be used with this system, but as I will explain later on, should be used in a particular order alongside TDM ones.

The most basic configuration (HD1) only uses a core card to host the mixer and I/O; it can also provide some TDM processing power. HD2 through HD7 use additional Accel cards to increase the amount of TDM processing as well as track and voice count.

Each card on the system can accommodate 32 inputs and outputs via the **Digidesign** 192 blue interfaces. As an example, an HD3 system consisting of one core card, two Accel cards, and six Digidesign 192 blue interfaces could accommodate 96 inputs and outputs.

Pro Tools HDX

The long-awaited replacement for HD Accel came up as HDX with upgraded **Field Programmable Gate Array (FPGA)** enabled cards and a new Avid Audio eXtensions plugin format that can run on both native (AAX) and accelerated (AAX-DSP) technologies. According to Avid's press release, a single card is comparable to five times the power of a TDM one, while the summing engine was upgraded to a 64-bit floating point and plugin processing to a 32-bit float for greater precision and headroom. The delay compensation engine was also increased to a maximum of 16,383 samples, enough to run the vast majority of plugins comfortably. For those too hungry for samples, we should use the audio suite instead.

The new AAX plugin format brings a better unification between HD and native systems. Before, RTAS and TDM plugins had to be coded differently, hence the sonic differences between the two. With AAX and AAX-DSP, the code can be ported from one to the other without any change, keeping the same sonic characteristics.

Because of the power increase and change in technology, HDX requires only one type of card. A single HDX will allow for 64 I/O, but its processing capabilities will also bring you enough power to run many AAX-DSP plugins and make most sessions happen entirely on an HDX 1 system.

Pro Tools HD Native

Pro Tools HD Native, like HDX, runs with a PCIE card but does not offer any processing power. Therefore, it is a light version of HDX that can only handle a maximum of 64 I/O because we cannot combine multiple HD Native cards together like we would with HDX. The chip handles input and output routing, allowing for low latency monitoring and to connect Avid interfaces. All other processing happens on the computer's CPU. It is also interesting to note that we can acquire HD native as an internal PCIE card or Thunderbolt external box.

Software options

The Pro Tools range has evolved quite a bit over the years. The most recent change to the Pro Tools software choice is the abandoning of LE versions. Now Pro Tools has three versions—Pro Tools Express, Pro Tools, and Pro Tools HD—each aimed at a different market. The latest release, Version 11, also saw the abandoning of the **Complete Production Toolkit**, which was a convenient upgrade path to many Pro Tools users who could not afford a full HD license.

Pro Tools HD 10/Pro Tools 10 with Complete Production Toolkit using third-party interfaces

It is possible to run an HD license on a native system (no cards) and still benefit from almost all the features. Purchasing the Complete Production Toolkit will also give you HD features from a standard Pro Tools license. Both rely solely on your CPU's processing power but rest assured that you will not loose any quality using another manufacturer's hardware; the summing engine is the same for HDX and all HD Native solutions except when using the latest Pro Tools 11.

 You might hear sonic changes, but they will be caused by the change of converters within the audio interface.

Mixing with this setup can work very well if you have a fast enough computer, but low latency monitoring will be limited to output 1 and 2 and will therefore be disabled for surround applications. More on low latency monitoring later in this chapter.

Pro Tools HD 10 or Pro Tools 10 with Complete Production Toolkit using Avid interfaces

Using an Avid interface will unlock the full capabilities of the software, speeding up the workflow by compensating automatically for hardware inserts as well as allowing low latency monitoring across all I/Os with or without AAX-DSP plugins for added recording or mixing power.

Pro Tools HD 11 update

The same rules apply when it comes to limitations using third-party interfaces, but the latest release of Pro Tools is a complete 64-bit rewrite of the application, increasing available system memory and performance. I will concentrate on the audio engine and what it means for us later, but just to give you an idea of how significant this update is, here are the highlights:

- A new audio engine (AAE for Avid Audio Engine).
- A new video engine (AVE for Avid Video Engine) that can harness the GPU power from your graphics card, freeing up the audio processing power when working with video. This new video engine is the same as Avid's professional video editing solution **Media Composer**.

- New track meters that can be calibrated to many industry standards, including the K-system and also new gain reduction meters with many different settings.

- An offline-bouncing feature that can also do multiexport and automatic MP3 creation.

- Double the number of undos — 64 instead of the previous 32.

- A new unified workspace browser.

- No more Complete Production Toolkit option for Pro Tools 11 owners; we now have to buy an HD license.

The new audio engine features three main improvements:

1. Full 64-bit float upgrade for a cleaner signal path, eliminating the need for conversion and therefore retaining maximum signal integrity all the time. This comes with drawbacks as Avid decided to drop all legacy code, including 32-bit plugins such as RTAS but also AAX 32-bit. The plugins will have to be coded either as AAX 64-bit or AAX-DSP 64-bit in order to be recognized by Pro Tools. RTAS, AAX 32-bit, AAX-DSP 32-bit, and AudioSuite 32-bit are no longer supported.

2. They also added a dynamic plugin-processing feature to maximize the plugin count and free up CPU usage if no audio is going through the plugin. This feature can improve system performance dramatically.

3. Finally, they allowed for a dual buffer technology, allowing different buffers to be used for armed-enabled tracks inside complex mixing sessions.

Buying Pro Tools HD 11 is therefore a move toward the future and will probably cost you more than just the software as third-party plugin developers will have to update their plugin to the new 64-bit standard. Most updates will come free, but some plugins might also never be ported. Luckily, Pro Tools 11 and Pro Tools 10 can coexist on the same machine; you even get a license for 10 when you buy 11, for backward compatibility.

Choosing the most adapted system

HDX with Pro Tools 11 is the best choice so far because it is the most powerful, accurate, and versatile system offering great software and hardware integration for tracking with AAX-DSP 64-bit plugins at an extremely low latency as well as extra processing power for mixing. HDX does not support old TDM plugins. Using HDX with Pro Tools HD 10 is still a very good option and offers a lot more plugin choices, but Pro Tools 11 will give you better sound quality as well as improved stability and processing power.

If you can find a bargain on the secondhand market, HD Accel is a potential alternative to HDX since it is a proven and reliable system; however, Avid will stop supporting it at the end of 2016. Like HDX, it will give the same processing advantages but with TDM plugins. AAX and AAX-DSP are not supported at all, and as we will discuss later, its audio resolution is not as well-developed as other solutions.

HD Native offers lower recording latency by offloading the routing processes to the PCIE card. This is beneficial for overall system performance while mixing or recording, but it will not allow any plugin processing to run on the chip, making this option a purely native platform. HD Native is therefore perfect if you would like to to perform mixing on your powerful desktop or laptop while being able to track at low latency.

If you already have an interface, you might want to keep it. A Pro Tools HD license will open with any interface. Pro Tools 10 with Complete Production Toolkit will give you the same benefits as any HD 10 user. Opting for Pro Tools 11 would also be very beneficial in this situation because of the overall performance and the new dual buffer option, which will still be able to track at acceptable latencies. Using a third-party interface will raise the overall latency slightly and Automatic Delay Compensation will not compensate for external inserts and external input monitoring automatically; we will later look at how to readjust the timing manually instead.

Recording and mixing considerations

Recording in a **Digital Audio Workstation** (**DAW**) can be subject to latency as the audio buffer takes time to be computed inside the digital domain resulting in a constant trade-off between increased stability (higher H/W buffer sizes) and lower latency (lower H/W buffer sizes). A very fast computer or more optimized and integrated DSP are very well equipped to handle low latencies. As we begin using native plugins while recording, the stress on the CPU can become too much for low buffer sizes. Increasing the playback engine's buffer will add more audio and MIDI latency, so an HDX or HD Accel system can help in solving this problem by allowing you to use DSP plugins instead. For this purpose, you need to use AAX-DSP or TDM plugins. These plugins will have much lower latencies than their native versions but at a higher price tag. One more thing to keep in mind is the sound difference between RTAS and TDM since the internal mathematics are different. We will learn more about their limitations later on, but as a general rule, working with the same plugin types will reduce audio representation changes and system usage.

DSP or no DSP?

So is it worth investing in an HD system? There are two different schools in the digital audio industry between DSP-accelerated systems and Native ones. Digital audio has been here since the advent of the modern computer. At first, CPUs were too slow to allow fast enough processing at low latencies, so DSP assistance was the way to go. Nowadays, CPUs have become so fast that additional DSP assistance is not necessarily the best solution as it can also add latency and complexity to the system. In many situations and projects, if you have a fast computer, you can probably do without the extra hardware.

 HDX cards are not the only way to get extra processing power. Universal Audio also uses DSP cards to run their plugins, adding power but a significant increase in latency, branding them as mixing plugins. This illustrates that it takes time for the signal to leave the CPU, get processed by the card, and come back to the CPU. Their latest Apollo soundcard solves this problem, embedding low latency DSP on the soundcard, and allows plugin processing at the time of recording.

If you understand their architectures, accelerated solutions still have many advantages over native solutions, but as CPUs become faster, the gap becomes smaller each year. The main advantage of an HDX or HD Accel system is their ability to run many more plugins using AAX DSP or TDM plugins at lower latency and higher track counts than a native-only system. They also allow you to track at low latency all the time because their cards handle audio processing. Your computer's CPU will also have a lot more resources for audio processing, so you should achieve greater performances, higher plugin counts, and improved stability on smaller systems.

Playback engine optimizations

Mixing internally or "in the box" depends on the type of audio engine we are using (floating, fixed, DSP, native) and an understanding of its internal routing and gain structure. Pro Tools 10, HDX, and HD Native have a 32-bit float processing engine and a double-precision, a 64-bit float summing engine, allowing for huge headroom and a lower noise flow than ever before. Pro Tools 11 takes it even further with a 64-bit floating point precision across the entire signal path.

Pro Tools HD 10 Playback Engine

Pro Tools' Playback Engine audio engine can be customized in many different ways by navigating to **Setup | Playback Engine**:

H/W Buffer Size

H/W Buffer Size sets how many samples the CPU processes at once, directly affecting the overall audio and MIDI latency. DAWs process audio in chunks of data representing a certain amount of samples. The lower the hardware buffer size, the less latency you will experience when monitoring audio, MIDI, and automations. On the other hand, a higher buffer size allows for more samples to be processed at once, increasing the native plugin count and overall latency. You can find your overall system latency or "**System Delay**" in **Setup | Session**.

Session window showing overall system delay

Host Processors and CPU Usage Limit

These parameters allocate a number of processors or virtual processors (depending on whether your computer supports hyper threading) to Pro Tools to process AAX and RTAS effects. On all native configurations. I recommend setting the host processor count to one unit less than the maximum at 99 percent usage limit, leaving one free unit for the operating system. Users can decrease those values to allocate more resources to other tasks such as video playback, automation, and general graphic work.

Delay Compensation engine

This option determines the maximum number of samples that can be compensated by **Automatic Delay Compensation (ADC)**. Since ADC grows with the project, it seems desirable to leave it at maximum (or Long if you are using HD Accel) if you are not looking at saving on unnecessary memory usage. ADC status is indicated by a "**Dly**" sign at the top of the edit window but is also activated or deactivated by navigating to **Option | Delay Compensation**. If the "**Dly**" sign turns red, you have exceeded the maximum delay duration and tracks will be out of time with each other.

Delay Compensation indicator

Disk Playback

Pro Tools 10 brought a new disk playback cache engine to HD and Complete Production Toolkit users, allowing sessions to be played back and recorded from RAM. This feature brought significant performance improvements. The normal setting streams audio files from your hard drive while choosing any of the available values and begins loading the session's audio files into RAM as shown in the **System Usage** window.

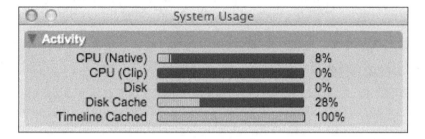

The Pro Tools HD 10 System Usage window

Disk Cache indicates how much of the disk cache allocation is currently used and **Timeline Cached** indicates how much of the **Edit** window is loaded into RAM. It can be very easy to overlook this option and begin to load too much and not leave enough for the system to operate properly, which results in poor performance. The use of a memory monitoring software can help you determine the best setting for your machine. You would be amazed to see how much code can stay loaded in RAM even after closing programs. If Pro Tools quits unexpectedly, unnecessary files can stay loaded in RAM, taking up space and impacting your next session. This is only some personal advice, but restarting your computer and/or cleaning the RAM every time a crash happens improves the overall system stability.

Plugin streaming buffer

The last option is related to the **Structure plugin**. If the plugin is installed, you will see a **Plug-In Streaming Buffer** option where you can set a manual or automatic cache size for streaming samples from the hard drive. Leave these options at the default setting (**Level 2**) unless you use many structure samples in your session and encounter playback issues.

With the new disk playback engine and the advance of solid state drives (SSD), it becomes less relevant to optimize a desktop computer with multiple hard drives. Mechanical hard drives are slow, even 7200 rpm ones; it is therefore good practice to use different hard drives for different applications such as the operating system, audio files, video files, and maybe even samples. By doing so, we can increase the system's performance and stability. I have been using Pro Tools 10 HD (with HD Native and also without Avid's hardware) with an upgraded SSD computer and noticed a pronounced improvement in overall performances, allowing me to reduce my hardware buffer size during recording and mixing over Pro Tools 9.

Voice allocation

An HDX or HD Accel system with Pro Tools HD 10 or HD 11 will also offer a voice configuration setting within the **Playback Engine** window. Voices are necessary to run and expand the Pro Tools mixer but also take DSP power, limiting resources for DSP plugins. Change this setting to best suit your needs.

Pro Tools 11 Playback Engine

Pro Tools 11 brought noticeable changes to the **Playback Engine** window and the way users can interact with it. Exit the host processor setting; Pro Tools will dynamically allocate all resources across all available processors. We also lost the **Plug-In Streaming Buffer** option and Automatic Delay Compensation settings, so there is less to worry about.

We only find **H/W Buffer Size** but it is not the same. In Pro Tools 10, this option refers to both input and playback buffer sizes as they were unified. In Pro Tools 11, this option refers to the input buffer size only, and the playback buffer size is automatically managed by Pro Tools. While this option affects both MIDI and audio data on all systems, it only affects tracks with native plugins on HDX systems.

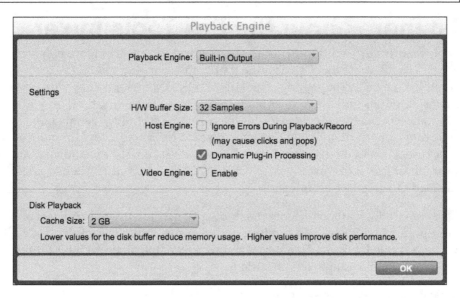

The new Playback Engine window for a native system

Pro Tools 11 changes are definitely major, and the new playback engine and audio engine have both been considerably upgraded and are a lot more user friendly. Those who have mixed with both HD Accel systems and the latest release, Version 11, should welcome the difference.

Automatic Delay Compensation (ADC)

ADC has been a long and painful story for Native users since Avid is still reluctant to embrace full native potential and currently works differently across different hardware and software versions. Here are the three different cases:

- Pro Tools HD Accel is limited to 4096 samples because of the hardware Accel card limitations. Since ADC requires memory, we can select three different ADC lengths from the **Playback Engine** window.

- Pro Tools 10 native or with HDX and HD Native hardware allows for 16,383 samples, which is also selectable from the **Playback Engine** window. Again, we are limited by HDX compatibility.

- Pro Tools 11 native or with HDX and HD Native hardware still has the same 16,383-sample limitation but no longer gives you the choice to select different ADC lengths. We can only disable or enable ADC from the **Option** menu.

A bit more about the Pro Tools mixer

Pro Tools features three different audio engines and each one of them behaves differently. To illustrate this let's assume that I am buying an old HD Accel system because it is financially interesting. The HD Accel TDM mixer comes with a few more considerations and drawbacks such as having to be very careful on your gain stage to maintain healthy levels as 24-bit fixed-point TDM plugins only have a dynamic range of 144 dB and can therefore discard information or clip more easily. In the next sections I will discuss some good practices and optimizations to make the most out of Pro Tools mixers. AAX-DSP, AAX Native, and RTAS use a 32-bit float instead of a fixed 24-bit integer.

First, let's have a look at the different technologies involved with Pro Tools and a bit about plugin architecture. In modern digital audio, audio is sampled at 24 bits integer per sample by the audio interface' converters, and since each bit represents 6 decibels of dynamic range, the formula is:

Dynamic Range (dB) = number of bits $\wedge$ 6

24 bits $\wedge$ 6 = 144 dB

Since each bit can have two states, 0 or 1, the maximum resolution of a system is based on the number of values that can be represented for each sample. In an integer environment it is given by:

Resolution = $2\wedge n$ (where n is the total number of bits)

$2\wedge 24$ = 16,777,216 values for a 24-bit system

So, in a 24-bit fixed point integer system, any number can be represented by one of the 16,777,216 values. One important limitation lies in the finite resolution of the representation. To illustrate this let's take the example of a 4-bit system, which gives 16 possible values ($2\wedge 4$). I can therefore represent number 0 to 15 in steps of 1. If I would like to represent 2.7, I cannot; I would have to round the result to the closest integer, adding distortion to the signal. After audio is sampled at 24-bit integer by the audio-to-digital converter (A/D), it is represented inside Pro Tools as 32-bit floating point for greater dynamic range representation and processing precision.

A 32-bit float system uses a 32-bit word made of a 24-bit mantissa to which we added an 8-bit exponent. While still using a 24-bit word, it has the ability to shift the exponent to represent the best possible value within the full 24-bit scale constraint, increasing the resolution and dynamic range of the system. While rounding errors also occur with floating point calculations, they are a lot smaller due to the increase in representation precision, especially for a 64-bit float.

As an example to better understand floating-point mathematics, we can represent a number in two different ways: 1,000 or 1 x 10^3. Here, "1" is called the mantissa and "10^3" the exponent. The sign can be stored using different methods that we will not discuss in this book.

With integer "fixed point" calculations, if the number of bits is exceeded, we either clip or lose low-level information. A floating point system can "float" its decimal to achieve optimum signal representation, shifting the 24-bit word up, losing low-level information if needed but avoiding clipping, or like in the following diagram, shifting it down to increase the dynamic range of the signal. So if a number falls outside the fixed range, it can be "floated" by having its decimal shifted to make use of all available bits of the 24-bit word.

The IEEE 754 standard defines the specifications for single-precision (32-bit float) and double-precision (64-bit float) computations. The dynamic range of floating point systems is very hard to quantify. The mathematics can have some surprising behaviors, and floating precision tends to lose precision in some cases. At first, many users were unsure whether integer or floating-point calculations are the best for audio-related tasks, even though the theoretical benefits are beyond any doubt. Both representations have advantages and disadvantages that we will not discuss further in this chapter because they are not relevant. However, I would like to state the generally accepted approximate dynamic range value of 1,500 dB for single-precision (32-bit float) and 12,300 dB for double-precision (64-bit float). Precision computation is a direct reflection of the mantissa's word length and is therefore greatly increased by 64-bit float processing.

Now that we understand better the fundamental differences between integer fixed point and floating point representations, the following diagram will illustrate how the TDM plugins interact with the Pro Tools mixer against their AAX-DSP, AAX, and RTAS counterparts.

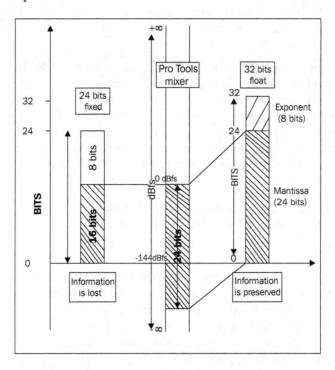

The preceding diagram represents the communication between the mixer and plugins. As shown, the left-hand side represents TDM, while the right-hand side of the diagram represents AAX-DSP/AAX/RTAS. When communicating with the internal mixer, information must be converted to floating point format. When coming from TDM fixed point calculation, information can be lost during the process; other formats will always retain full 24-bit of dynamic range.

When using AAX 32-bit, AAX-DSP 32-bit, or RTAS plugins, the 16- or 24-bit audio file is represented using a 32 bit float resolution at every sample, processed internally at higher resolution or not. It is then returned to the 32-bit float insert and summed with other signals inside the 64-bit float mixer using a 32-bit float resolution inserts on the master output tracks. We now begin to understand that there is a lot of conversion going on there, effectively "coloring" our signal.

If you are using HDX or HD Accel, it gets a bit more complicated. With AAX-DSP, same as native, everything stays at 32-bit floats, but with TDM, we use a 24-bit fixed integer. The signal can still be treated using higher resolution internally, but the plugin output will be returned to 24-bit to be mixed inside the 48-bit fixed point mixer. We can also use RTAS on an Accel system so more conversion steps can be involved when chaining different plugin types one after the other.

Floating point representation gives you enough headroom not to worry about clipping, but with a 24-bit fixed, anything below -144 dBfs will be lost and anything above 0 dBfs will be clipped. It becomes really important to be fully aware of those TDM limitations. The same applies for RTAS plugins used within an HD Accel environment since the 48-bit mixer communicates with plugins on a 24-bit bus. If you are using HD Accel, here are two good ways to do it:

- Use master faders and watch the track meter to adjust bus levels before entering any plugin on the bus or on the audio track.
- Look at the plugin clip indicator by looking at your channel strip. If any plugin' name is displayed in red, it has been clipped.

If using any other system, clip indicators inside the plugin might light up, but if the plugin is internally coded in 32-bit floats or higher, you can stack as many plugins as you like without ever needing to clip the audio, even if the internal meter shows clipping. On the other hand, even if you hear no distortion, it is also good practice to control your gain stage so you can also use these as mixing references.

Pro Tools 11 goes further, upgrading processing to 64-bit, which according to IEEE standards, is composed of one sign bit, a 52-bit mantissa, and an 11-bit exponent. That means even greater precision across the mixer and greater headroom than 32-bit floats. A 64-bit float precision increases fidelity across the entire signal chain, eliminating the need for signal representation changes. It has greater mantissa precision and enough dynamic range for you to never hear any audible distortion, and the signal will be very precise. Only the master output faders can show audible clipping as they represent the signal being sent to the digital-to-audio converters (D/A), which are 24-bit integers.

A 32-bit float was great but Pro Tools 11 takes audio fidelity to the next level by increasing the dynamic range and precision even further as well as by taking away all the unnecessary signal conversion along the entire signal path.

Voices and time slots

Voices are audio connection points between your CPU and the DSP, they represent audio tracks. Time slots or "Timeslots" mean two different things:

For HD Accel they represent connections not only within the DSP but also from the CPU or to the physical outputs of your interface, much like a patch bay. Timeslot numbers are fixed to 512 to move audio within the Pro Tools mixer, including TDM plugins. We can appreciate how fast their number can grow and possibly limit the system.

For HDX, they represent connection between multiple HDX cards meaning that an HDX1 system do not require any timeslots. This is because HDX uses new FPGA technology, moving away from full TDM architecture. The improved 1,536 timeslots TDM bus is only used to communicate between cards.

Pro Tools HD Accel has a maximum of 192 voices; HDX increases this number to 768. Under normal use, a mono track is equal to one voice, which means as long as you stay within the DSP domain. Once an audio stream is transferred into the Pro Tools mixer, it can leave the DSP via the interface or the track inserts for RTAS or AAX native processing. The latest option requires extra voices because we are moving back and forth from DSP, so we should be careful not to insert native plugins after DSP ones. As long as you respect this order, maximum efficiency can be achieved. Inside the playback engine setup, we can choose between different voicing settings. There will always be a combination of amount of voices to play back the tracks against available DSP usage for plugin processing.

 Time slots and voice counts are related to the sample rate. A higher sample higher than 48 kHz will bring down the number of voices and time slots available.

Here are some insert signal flow examples for a mono signal, to show how different arrangements can bring extra voice usage:

- RTAS/AAX → AAX-DSP/TDM → Output = 1 voice
- RTAS/AAX → AAX-DSP/TDM → RTAS/AAX → Output = 3 voices
- Hardware inserts take two voices
- An auxiliary input to a physical output takes one voice
- An auxiliary return from a physical output takes one voice

Master faders and auxiliary tracks without any native plugin do not require any voicing.

Low latency monitoring (LLM) and cue mixes

When it comes to keeping everything in the box, we are always fighting with latency. Even mixing can be unresponsive when using MIDI controllers with large buffer sizes. The normal production process usually begins with recording, followed by adding plugins, and mixing later on. Sometimes recording an overdub within a busy mix session is required and can have different strategies depending on which Pro Tools setup we are using.

When working with accelerated systems such as HDX or Accel, we do not have to worry about setting up anything as all routing and audio processing is handled by the DSP; the latency is kept low when used with DSP plugins only. This is because only native plugins have to use the playback engine buffer; AAX-DSP or TDM plugins run natively on the HDX or Accel cards at low latencies all the time.

With all native solutions, the CPU handles the mixer and processing, so everything goes through the CPU H/W buffer, and therefore, any armed track will be affected by an increase in monitoring latency. Pro Tools provides a dedicated low latency monitoring option that can be configured from two different locations depending on what hardware you are using. For all systems, the feature can be enabled or disabled from the **Option** menu. For Avid-accelerated systems it is also configurable from **Setup | I/O | Outputs**.

 LLMs do not work if the track output is assigned to an internal bus. It has to be routed directly to the default 1 and 2 or user defined outputs.

Any native plugin and active auxiliary send associated with the track will be disabled.

Different native solutions offer different options as follows:

- When using an HD Native card with Pro Tools HD 10 with a high H/W buffer size, we have to use the low latency monitoring mode. This option allows the user to choose a desired output number and route any track assigned to this output only, so they will be routed directly from within the DSP card instead, thus bypassing any plugin on the track. It is also important to understand that LLM works by muting the record armed track output only during recording, so you will still be able to perform punch in and overdubs.

- When using Pro Tools HD 10 or equivalent with third-party interfaces, LLM will be limited to a single-stereo output that cannot be changed: output 1 and 2. You will also need to make sure that your soundcard has an onboard virtual mixer to route the desired signal to output 1 and 2, or you will hear nothing during recording as LLM mutes software monitoring while recording.
- With Pro Tools HD 11, the same rules apply when using LLM; the only change is that we have another option with the dual-buffer technology. If you manage to set it low enough, it is the most convenient way of performing any overdub and you will not need to use LLM.

Now, when it comes to creating a cue mix with LLM engaged in either HD 11 or 10, the traditional way of creating an internal aux send mix to a separate output is not possible anymore unless we own an HD Native card, so we can select a different LLM output other than our mix output. When using third-party interfaces, we have no choice but to create the cue mix from within the soundcard mixer.

Pro Tools version summary

Pro Tools is a complex system with many different versions of the hardware and software and Version 10, offering a dual-installation method, will be the last version to support legacy TDM plugins alongside RTAS. Pro Tools 11 abandoned all legacy code and technologies to create a much more accurate signal path. To recapitulate what we have seen so far, here is a comparative table:

	HDX 1 with HD 10	HD Accel 3 with HD10	HD Native with HD10	PT10 + CPTK with third party interface	PT HD 11 with Avid HDX1 or HD Native
Voices	256 to 768	192	256	256	256 to 768
Timeslots	1,536	512	1,536	1,536	1,536
Max I/O	64	96	64	32	64
DSP plugins	AAX DSP	TDM	No	No	Yes
Processing resolution	32-bit float	24-bit fixed	32-bit float	32-bit float	64-bit float
Mixer resolution	64-bit float	48-bit fixed	64-bit float	64-bit float	64-bit float
Automatic ADC on hardware	Yes	Yes	Yes	No	Yes

	HDX 1 with HD 10	HD Accel 3 with HD10	HD Native with HD10	PT10 + CPTK with third party interface	PT HD 11 with Avid HDX1 or HD Native
Low Latency Monitoring	Yes	Yes	Yes	Limited to output 1 and 2	Yes
ADC max	16,383	4,095	16,383	16,383	16,383
Pro Tools application	32-bit	32-bit	32-bit	32-bit	64-bit
Pro video engine	No	No	No	No	Yes

Customizing MIDI

Pro Tools uses Audio MIDI Setup on Mac and MIDI Studio Setup on Windows computers to generate a list of MIDI devices. In this section I will show you how to make a custom MIDI device and how to use an external hardware such as a software synthesizer.

Organizing external MIDI devices

If you are using a MIDI interface with multiple ports, you might have some devices permanently connected to some of the ports. In this example, I will create a new external MIDI device attached to my MIDI interface port so that Pro Tools can show it directly inside the software. Here are the steps to create a custom MIDI instrument:

1. Open the MIDI studio by navigating to **Setup | MIDI | MIDI Studio**.

2. Audio MIDI Setup (on Mac) or MIDI Studio Setup (on Windows) opens.

3. Create a new device in either one of them.

4. Rename it with the device's name. In my case, this is **Moog Voyager**.

5. Connect the virtual ins and outs of the device to the correct port.

If you now open a Pro Tools MIDI track, you can select "**Moog Voyager**" from **Audio MIDI Setup (AMS)** on Mac or **MIDI Studio Setup (MSS)** on Windows.

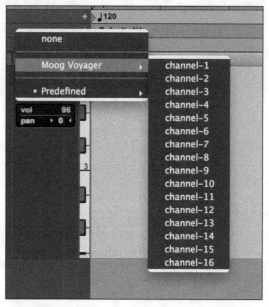

The Pro Tools MIDI list mirroring AMS or MSS showing the Moog Voyager

There is no limit to how many instruments you can have, only the number of MIDI ports on your computer's interface.

 You can also create different instruments on the same MIDI port using different MIDI channels. In Audio MIDI Setup or MIDI Studio Setup, you can specify on which channels each virtual device operates.

Controlling MIDI hardware on instrument tracks

On a regular instrument track, the MIDI input gets off your computer master keyboard and is routed to the first plugin in the insert chain. But few users know that we can route the master keyboard to an external MIDI output (**Moog Voyager**), recording its MIDI output and monitoring it by selecting the corresponding audio input on the track.

To display the instrument track section, click on the edit window view selector and select **Instruments** or navigate to **View | Edit Window Views** or **Mix Window Views | Instruments**.

1. In the instrument section, select the desired MIDI input for your master keyboard.

2. Also in the instrument section, select a MIDI output for the MIDI instrument.

3. Now select audio input for the track.

The hardware MIDI instrument can now be played like any other AAX or RTAS software instrument and can record MIDI and process the audio on the same track. Once done, record the audio to a new audio track.

Routing using a Moog used as a virtual instrument

Plugin mapping and MIDI learn

In Pro Tools some plugins support MIDI learn functionalities internally, whereas others don't. Instead of MIDI learn, Pro Tools also offers an internal plugin mapping feature that is limited to Avid/Digidesign controllers such as ICON, S6, Command|8, and C|24. If a compatible controller is connected, the mapping option will show at the top of the **Plugin** window. Using Avid controllers over standard MIDI protocols is a significant workflow and resolution advantage as Avid developed its software and hardware integration really well over the past years. We have two main scenarios:

• If you are using an unsupported MIDI control surface, you will be limited to the plugins supporting internal MIDI learn functions. All you have to do is make sure that the MIDI input device is recognized in MIDI Studio and declare it in: **Setup | MIDI | Input Devices**.

• If you own a supported MIDI controller such as the Command|8, we can use both MIDI learn and plugin mapping but must also declare it in **Setup | Peripherals | MIDI Controllers**.

To map a plugin with a supported control surface:

1. Click on the **Learn** button above the **Plugin** window; it will light up red.
2. Select the plugin parameter.
3. Select the desired encoder on the control surface.

From the **Map** drop-down menu at the top of the **Plugin** window, you can also perform many different actions, for example, Save, Export, Use as Default, Rename, and so on.

Summary

In this chapter we learned that there are a lot more Pro Tools range than it seems, and we are currently experiencing a transition period from a 32-bit to full a 64-bit architecture. We also implemented and configured MIDI devices to improve our workflow. In the next chapter we will look at editing techniques for drums and vocals to enhance and be more creative with recorded performances.

2

Editing Techniques

In this chapter, we will look at how to make better use of Pro Tools' editing tools and techniques. Editing is a very important part of today's music productions tools and can be used to improve, clean, rearrange, correct, and even get creative with the performance.

Vocal editing preparations

Vocal editing is an essential skill for any producer or engineer and Pro Tools offers few settings that we should configure before going any further.

First let's not forget to disable the **Link Timeline and Edit Selection** and **Insertion Follows Playback** options, to be able to modify the waveform without losing the timeline selection and be able to press stop/play and audition from the same start point.

We should also disable window scrolling by selecting **None** from **Option | Edit Window Scrolling**.

Insertion Follows Playback/Link Timeline and Edit Selection

 The following shortcuts can be used:
Link Timeline and Edit Selection: *Shift + /*
Insertion Follow Playback: *N*

Zero crossing

Editing vocal in Pro Tools can be a bit tricky, since the software does not provide a "snap to zero crossing" option. Therefore, every time we make a cut on an audio clip, we are at a risk of creating a click like the example below:

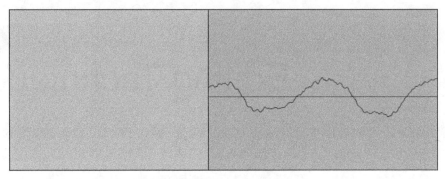

A typical click as a result of clip cut

To avoid clicks, we can perform either of the following:

- Manually cut at zero crossing:

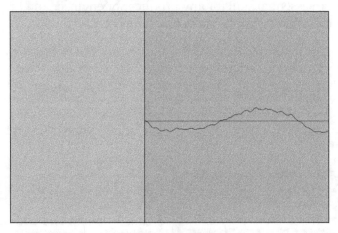

A cut at zero crossing

- Create a fade:

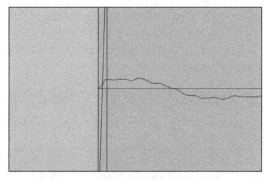

Fade to avoid click

There is another option if we are looking at doing some quick editing without being too self-conscious about our cuts; we can use the clip auto fade option by navigating to **Preferences | Operation | Misc**. Here, we can adjust the length of the fade in milliseconds. The fades will not show up on the clips, but will be bounced with the **Bounce To Disk** feature. Because this is an automatic option, we should also try a few settings and audition the project because even very fast fades can affect the feel of a drum performance.

Clip auto fades settings are local and saved with our project, so we can adjust this option without affecting other projects.

Because it is a real-time feature, we have to use the **Bounce To Disk** feature to render Automatic Fades. AudioSuite and clip consolidation will not render any of them.

Relative grid

Many clicks arise while editing directly on the grid, but the waveform is almost never in the right place unless we are working with pre-edited samples. Let's say that I have edited a few vocal recordings for chorus 1, and I would like to copy them to chorus 2. The problem is that my audio clip is beginning slightly before the grid. We could separate the clips on the grid, move them, and then drag the beginning of the clip to recover the entire waveform. This technique is very time consuming. Let's use a relative grid instead. To enable relative grid, press the *F4* key to toggle between **Grid** and **Relative Grid**.

Relative grid moves clips across the **Edit** window keeping their relative position to the grid instead of snapping to every grid subdivisions. So if a clip is beginning 20 ms before a grid subdivision, moving it or copying it across the project will keep it at the same relative position from any other subdivision. Once selected, we can copy and paste clips to the next chorus without having to worry about timing issues; everything will be where it should.

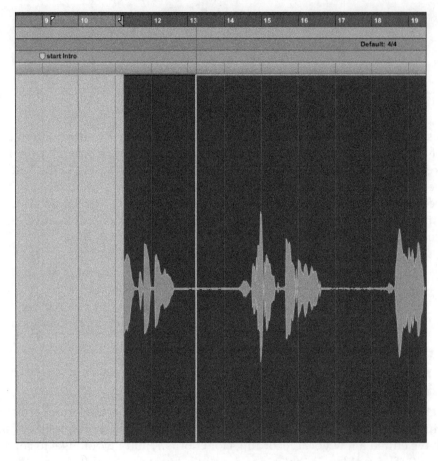

Notice the clip beginning and the thick yellow line where the clip will be dragged. They keep their relative position to the grid.

Finding clicks

A good way to identify the correct track is to use solo modes. Pro Tools offers three options: **Latch**, **X-OR**, and **Momentary**, all of which are accessible from the **Solo mode** menu present in the **Option** tab. **Latch** will retain the previously soloed track, hence I find **X-OR** and **Momentary** the most useful ones since they do not latch. I can then quickly solo one track after the other and find the click.

Now that we have found the track, let's find the click. Clicks are transient and can occur in multiple forms on the waveform. Pops are a similar issue but would have a much lower frequency. They can be created by bad editing, mouth clicks on vocals, analog behavior, plugin automations (we will not see this on the waveform), or be a part of the sound, like on a kick. But in most vocal cases, we would want to take them out to improve the performance's quality and clarity.

> To zoom faster on the desired part of the project, make an edit selection and press *option + F* (Mac) or *Alt + F* (Windows), to fit the entire selection on the screen. Another great way of soloing tracks is by using the **Link Track and Edit Selection** option; that is, quickly move up and down with *P* and *;* and then use the *Shift + S* shortcut keys to solo.

An easy way to find a click on the waveform is to look for fast transients or use the scrubber tool to audition. The scrubber tool, like when working a vinyl, allows us to drag the playback head at custom speed while auditioning the audio. It is handy for many applications like clicks and timing checks. To select the scrubber tool, toggle the *F6* key.

As an alternative to the scrubber tool, we can hold the *control* key (Mac) or the Start key (Windows) and drag onto the clip with the selection tool or the smart tool. But with the latest option, we have to position the cursor in the top part of the clip. When the cursor turns into a speaker, we are ready to audition.

Audition until we find the click, Press *F7* for the selection tool, select the desired range, and press *option + F* to fit the selection to the entire screen. There are two ways to deal with clicks: repair them or remove them.

Repairing a click using the pencil tool is very easy and should be used as much as possible since it is the most discrete option. It is also a destructive edit, so we should create a new audio file of the portion to edit with the consolidated features by pressing *option* + *shift* + *3* (Mac) or *Alt* + *Shift* + *3* (Windows). The pencil tool can be very tedious at first, but there is no equivalent to it.

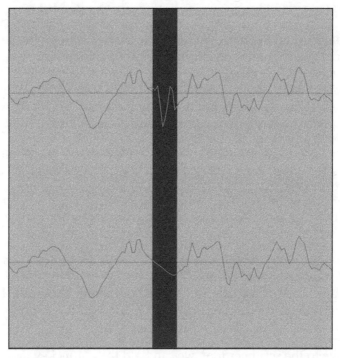

Repairing a click with the pencil tool. Original waveform (top) and after pencil editing (bottom).

Sometimes, it is desirable to correct a longer part of the audio file. In the next example, a few pops and mouth clicks are present on the silent part. We could remove that part altogether or copy paste the audio in order to keep the background noise consistent. Since this is a quiet middle eight, I will replace that part with another and crossfade them.

Downloading the color images of this book

We also provide you a PDF file that has color images of the screenshots/diagrams used in this book. The color images will help you better understand the changes in the output. You can download this file from http://www.packtpub.com/sites/default/files/downloads/8160OT_Graphics.pdf.

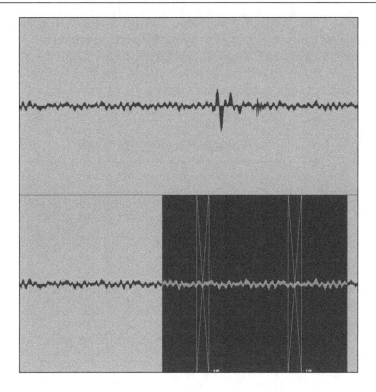

Removing low level pop or replacing it with another portion of audio. Before (top) and after replacing the audio (bottom).

Cuts and fades

Cuts and fades are used all the time to improve performances and remove unwanted parts. We can cut and fade in different ways to give different feels. In this example, I will show some techniques that can improve a vocal performance.

The Fades window

This window offers a few important settings. Fades can be created two ways: by dragging the top clip corner with the smart tool, or by making a selection and pressing *command* + *F* (Mac) or *Ctrl* + *F* (Windows). Open the **Fades** window by double-clicking on the fade itself.

The most important option for us is the slope settings. **Equal Power** and **Equal Gain** will create two different types of curves. While this option can be creative for fades, it is most important for crossfades; **Equal Power** is more suited for different signals, and **Equal Gain** for similar material. In our case, we would choose the **Equal Gain** option to crossfade the vocals together.

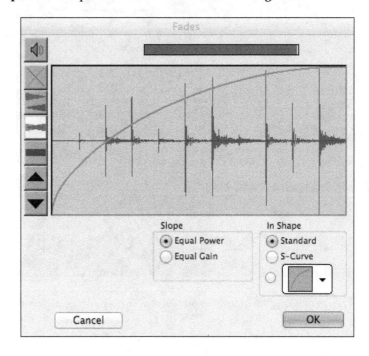

The Fades window

Every time we create a fade or crossfade, Pro Tools will follow the default settings from **Preferences | Editing**. From this window, we can edit those settings; this is very useful when coming back to the same fade over and over.

Linear fades (**Equal Gain**) and logarithmic fades (**Equal Power**) sound a lot different. When it comes to editing vocals, using one or the other type can change the performance. I like using fades to smooth out breathing, adjust performance, and clean up tracks. Many singers breathe heavily right before singing. This can be very unpleasant during the performance, especially when high compression and make up gain is applied. In most cases, we would just cut the breathing altogether, but sometimes it sounds more natural to keep it. A quick fade before the line can make a real difference to the performance.

I like using **Equal Power** with rhythmic vocals because they rise and fall faster, whereas linear fades can be more suited for quiet or more melodic passages. Choosing fade settings appropriately can be very beneficial.

Cutting can also be very useful. Sometimes, busy arrangements require very tight timing in order to make space for other instruments. A typical chorus line with rhythmical singing can almost always be improved by cutting in between the words. While this might sound unnatural at first, within the mix, it will not be perceived in the same way (especially if using reverbs or delays which create artificial tails) and create invaluable space for other instruments to improve the general performance and clarity. In fact, this has been turned into an effect and we can hear the effect of this technique all the time; especially in dance music. As an example, I have a vocal line where the singer is breathing a bit too heavily between words, but this might as well be any other unpleasant sound, such as the background noise. Everything makes a difference and even small tiny details like a breath can take away the impact and clarity of many background instruments. By cutting in between, we can enhance the overall performance.

> Creating many different clips can add extra workload on the CPU and graphics card, redrawing more and rendering more fades. A good trick at the end of our editing is to copy the edited clips to a new playlist and consolidate this newly created playlist, so we can always go back to the edit if needed. To consolidate clips, make an edit selection and press *option + shift + 3* (Mac) or *Alt + Shift + 3* (Windows). Consolidate works across multiple tracks by selecting in the **Edit** window.

For quicker manual editing, the **Fade to Start** or **Fade to End** options are also very useful; here are their shortcuts:

	Mac	Windows
Fade to Start	*option + D*	*Alt + D*
Fade to End	*option + G*	*Alt + G*

Clip gain

Clip gain is a new feature of Pro Tools 10. It allows changing the audio gain from the clip itself. This can be beneficial in many ways: speeding up workflow by not having to create complex automations instead; as a fade alternative for complex envelopes and giving us more control over compression plugins placed after on the inserts. The signal flow is as follows: Clip gain → Track Inserts → Track volume faders.

Clip gain comes in two styles: a general clip gain at the bottom left of the clip and a clip gain line to create complex breakpoint envelopes. To display the clip gain settings, navigate to **View | Clip**, and select **Clip Gain Line** or **Clip Gain Info**. We can also right-click on a clip and select from the **Clip Gain** menu or use the shortcuts explained a little bit later in this chapter.

Using clip gain, we can create more complex envelopes and because they are as editable as any other automation, we can use the smart tool and modifier keys to copy clip gain (*control + shift + C* on a Mac or Start + *Shift + C* on Windows) and paste it using the regular paste shortcut. This can lead to better and faster sound design effects, using the shape tool to create repetitive patterns.

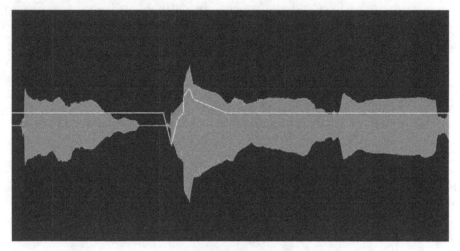

Complex clip gain envelope

Here is an essential shortcut for the smart tool modifier, which can be used for many other edits:

- *command* + click (Mac) or *Ctrl* + click (Windows): add marker points
- *option* + click (Mac) or *Alt* + click (Windows): remove marker points

 As a general rule of thumb, *command/Ctrl* modifies the default tool state and *option/Alt* makes the opposite action.

To trim a clip gain, make a selection with the smart tool and place it on the clip gain line (when the cursor changes to a horizontal line), then use the trim function by holding the clip and dragging it up or down.

We can create gradual changes by holding the *Shift* key while trimming the clip gain, but we have to make sure to create breakpoints outside the area first.

The **Clip Gain Nudge Value** option found by navigating to **Pro Tools Preferences |
Editing** allows nudging an entire clip gain by the user-defined increment. You will
find more clip gain shortcuts under the shortcut list within the **Help** menu, but here
are the ones I use most often:

	Mac	Windows
Show/hide clip gain line	*control* + *shift* + -	Start + *Shift* + -
Show/hide clip gain	*control* + *shift* + =	Start + *Shift* + =
Nudge up/down clip gain	*control* + *shift* + Up or Down arrow	Start + *Shift* + Up or Down arrow
Nudge forward/backward clip gain	*control* + *shift* + - or +	Start + *Shift* + - or +
Copy/cut	*control* + *shift* + C or X	Start + *Shift* + C or X
Clear	*control* + *shift* + B	Start + *Shift* + B
Paste	*command* + V	*Ctrl* + V

Elastic Audio

Manipulating a vocal performance is becoming a very easy job using Elastic Audio.
Introduced in Pro Tools 7.4, Elastic Audio is a powerful tool for time-stretching
audio, especially vocal. There are currently three ways of correcting vocal timing
with Pro Tools:

- Separate clips and move them manually around the timeline using the
  mouse or the nudge function
- Separate clips and time stretch them using the **Time Compression
  Expansion (TCE)** tool
- Use Elastic Audio

Separating, clips can be just what we need; however, in some cases, they can sound
very unnatural in quiet passages.

The TCE tool is most convenient when a single word falls too short or too long;
however, TCE fails at solving complex time stretching. Using this tool we can select
different TCE algorithms and settings by navigating to **Preferences | Processing**.
Pro Tools comes with some TCE plugins, but also supports algorithms from other
manufacturers. Check the TCE options by navigating to Preferences | Processing |
TC/E to select and choose available plugins.

Elastic Audio is the most convenient of the three techniques because it allows for
subtle and also more complex time stretching changes in audio files in a much more
user-friendly way. To enable Elastic Audio, select an algorithm from the Elastic
Audio Plugin Selector in the **Edit** window track header.

The selector gives us the choice between **Polyphonic**, **Rhythmic**, **Monophonic**, **Varispeed**, and **X-Form**. They can all (except **X-Form**) be used in real time, but they can all be used offline (rendered) too.

Depending on which plugin is selected, we can adjust its options. To display the **Option** window, just click on the track's Elastic Audio plugin selector's header. There are no golden settings, the defaults almost always work well but fine-tuning parameters will make you wonder why you never tried before. Here is a summary of the different available plugins:

	Polyphonic	Rhythmic	Monophonic	Varispeed	X-Form
Real-time	Yes	Yes	Yes	Yes	No
Options	• Follow • Window size	• Decay rate	No	No	• Quality • Formant
Best for	All polyphonic material	Rhythmic and transient audio	Monophonic sources (vocals, synth, bass, and so on)	• Everything where pitch is not a concern • Effects	Everything

Correcting vocal with Elastic Audio includes the following steps:

1. Select **Monophonic** from the Elastic Audio plugin list.

2. Select **Analysis** from the track view selector and create or correct markers to be at the important places, such as beginning of words or transients.

   1. Once the analysis is complete, with the smart tool, double-click on the clip to create a marker, hold *option* (Mac) or *Alt* (Windows) to remove markers.

   2. With the pencil tool, click to create, press *option* (Mac) or *Alt* (Windows) to remove the marker.

3. Select **Warp** from the track view selector. With the smart tools, double-click on an analysis marker from the bottom half of the clip to transform it into a warp marker. Hold *option* (Mac) or *Alt* (Windows) to remove it.

4. Dragging a warp marker will stretch the audio before and after the marker to the next one, so it is necessary to activate one before and after or create new ones or activate the existing ones to anchor the audio in the right place. Holding the *Shift* key while dragging a warp marker will automatically activate the analysis markers in the neighborhood for you.

X-form is the only non real-time plugin and should be used for final processing. It takes quite some time to compute (especially with the best quality settings), but after that it does not take any processing power. If you would like to stick to the real-time algorithm but still render them, just select **Rendered Processing** from the Elastic Audio plugin selector. To commit Elastic Audio processing to the audio file, just select **None** from the Elastic Audio plugin selector and then select **Commit**.

Using AudioSuite

AudioSuite, accessible from the **AudioSuite** menu, is a Pro Tools offline plugin format, which allows to process clips without sacrificing processing power. I use AudioSuite all the time to process a small portion of audio, such as individual syllables, to balance my frequency content. Recording with any type of cardioid or figure of eight microphones will bring a varying amount of proximity effect. This can be desirable to enhance the low frequency content of a vocal or play with the effect to add sound texture to the voice, but most often, many singers begin their line too close to the microphone, adding an unnecessary amount of low end.

In most situations, we could just reduce the level of the affected part by separating the clip and using the gain plugin to create a crossfade; we could also create a fade. Using clip gain is a much more convenient way of performing those kinds of edit tasks, but in most cases, I prefer applying a high-pass filter to the audio file with AudioSuite.

As an example, if our first plugin is a compressor, the proximity effect can trigger a lot more compression, so it is better to reduce it directly from the audio file. On an aesthetic side, breathing with low end in it sounds very heavy, so filtering those portions can also add to the "breathiness" of the performance and make the vocal lighter. I also use this technique for vocal matching after comping Some takes might sound slightly different from one others, often within the reach of a few dBs on the equalizer.

To use AudioSuite, make an edit selection and select the AudioSuite plugin from the **AudioSuite** menu. We can open multiple AudioSuite plugins by holding the *Shift* key.

When using AudioSuite, the selected portion of the clip will be separated and a new audio file (and related clip) will be created on top. If we need to crossfade after or before the edit, Pro Tools 10 has introduced a new "handle" feature, which greatly improves the AudioSuite workflow by processing the audio outside the edit selection, so we can trim the beginning and ending of a clip after processing. The length of those handles can be customized by navigating to **Preferences** | **Processing**. We can either choose a defined length or process the entire file every time we use AudioSuite.

> We can also adjust the handle length from the bottom of the
> **AudioSuite** window.

Once we have defined the default handle settings, we should make sure that our audition path is set correctly in **Setup | I/O | Outputs | Audition Path**. AudioSuite audition can therefore be rooted to any output of the audio interface.

One of the AudioSuite flaws is its inability to provide a processing history; processing the same clip or edit selection many times over will replace the audio clip every time. It is then difficult to revert back to the previous version. One workaround is to create a new playlist for each processing, but this process can be tedious. Right now, the only way to recover the original audio file is by finding it inside the clip list. Each AudioSuite processing will add AS (plugin name abreviation) to the original clip name. The following screenshot is a lead vocal example I processed with the Avid Channel Strip:

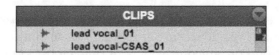

Using the AudioSuite plugin can also be slow and tedious if we repeatedly use the same processing over and over. Many times when I find a good setting, I tend to re-use it. Pro Tools can help on this side with the **Window Configuration List**:

1. Display favorite AudioSuite plugin (we can display multiple plugins by holding the *Shift* key when selecting a plugin).

2. Modify settings as per preference and navigate to **Window | Configuration** and click on **New Configuration**.

3. Name it, select **Window Layout** and click on **OK**.

4. We can now access this configuration via the **Window Configuration List** option (*command + option + J* on Mac or *Ctrl + Alt + J* on Windows).

5. Now, every time we recall a configuration, AudioSuite plugins will be shown with their settings as well as the entire window layout.

>
>
> To recall a window configuration, on the numeric keypad, press .,
> then type the window configuration number followed by *.
> For example, . 8 *.
>
> Even though window configurations are stored with our session,
> we can transfer them via the import session data function from
> **File | Import | Session Data** (*option + shift + I* on Mac or *Alt +
> Shift + I* on Windows).

Take comping

Pro Tools comping features are very well implemented and with a bit of preparation, we can really speed up workflow as well as improve any vocal performance easily and creatively. First, let's make sure to match playlist numbers and take count. Let me explain.

If I create an audio track called Vocal and begin recording on it, my first clip will be called Vocal_01. Now I create a new playlist and my second take will have the suffix 01 to reflect the playlist number 1, which in reality should be called playlist number 2.

This is because Avid thought that the first take should be the comp (or main playlist), and therefore, take 1 should be recorded on playlist 1. To avoid any confusion, at the recording stage, we should first create a new playlist and begin recording there.

> Create new playlist shortcut for the first selected track or grouped tacks:
>
> *control* + \ (Mac) or *Start* + \ (Windows)

We now have matching take numbers and automatic playlist numbering. This will remove a lot of confusion during the recording and also make the note taking process easier. Another way of keeping track of the best takes is to use clip rating. Each clip can be given a rating of 1 to 5, corresponding to our own interpretation. For me, 5 is a keeper.

- To rate a clip, select it and navigate to **Clip | Rating** or, use the shortcut *command + option + control* and number *1* to *5* on Mac. On Windows, press *Ctrl* + *Start* + *Alt*.

- To display clip rating navigate to **View | Clip | Rating**.

> For faster compositing, use the **Separate Clips Operates on All Related Takes** option available in **Preferences | Editing | Clips**. This will separate all the related takes with the same user timestamps.

By default, Pro Tools will play the main playlist. To audition the alternate playlists, click on their solo button. Now a good trick to solo the different playlists is to use a few key commands:

1. On the main playlist, make the edit selection with **Link Timeline and Edit Selection** enabled for the section we would like to replace.

2. Select **Loop Playback** (number *4* on the numeric keypad).

3. Navigate to the playlist below by pressing *;*, or above with *P*.

4. Solo the take with *Shift + S* and **Link Track and Edit Selection** enabled.

5. To promote the best take to the main playlist, just press *option + control + V* (Mac) or *Alt + Start + V* (Windows). We can also press the up arrow icon next to the solo button.

Drum editing

Drum editing is also a very nice skill to develop. Ever since I have been an engineer, Pro Tools has always been in the lead in this type of work because of its very good group editing features and Beat Detective. Beat Detective is a very good and versatile tool and we will see some its advanced uses later in this chapter.

With Pro Tools 7.4, we saw the arrival of Elastic Audio, which had a very different approach than Beat Detective, using time stretching algorithms to make editing audio feel a lot more like MIDI. But as always, first, let's see how we can organize ourselves better to edit drums more comfortably.

Edit and Mix groups

When it comes to editing drums, we usually work with quite a few tracks, so grouping becomes really important. Pro Tools offers three kinds of groups: **Edit**, **Mix**, and **Mix/Edit**.

Creating a group is easy; just select the tracks from the **Edit** or **Mix** window and press *command + G* (Mac) or *Ctrl + G* (Windows). The **Create Group** window opens and contains the following options:

- **Attributes**: Choose the group type you would like to create. To edit drums, I would choose to create an **Edit** group, but I could also choose **Mix/Edit**. The ID number is the letter we can use when our key focus is on the group window to enable or disable the group. VCA allows us to assign a VCA track to a **Mix** group. We will see more about VCA mixing in the next chapter.

> To toggle keyboard focus between **Edit** (1), **Mix** (2), and **Group** (3) window, use the following key commands:
>
> On Mac: *command + option* and keyboard numbers *1* to *3*.
>
> On Windows: *Ctrl + Alt* and keyboard numbers *1* to *3*.

- **Tracks**: Within this tab, we are able to choose the track that will be part of the group. One track can be part of multiple groups. The **Edit** group always follows the global attribute from the **Global** tab; **Mix** and **Edit/Mix** groups can either follow the global attribute, or have their own from the **Attributes** tab. To enable or disable global attributes, click on **Follow Global**.

- **Global**: These attributes can follow many configuration settings and combinations. We can save up to six different templates from the bottom of the window. We can also select different track settings to link for **Track Inserts** on the left of the window and **Track Sends** on the right.

    - **Track Insert** allows linking plugin parameter controls as well as bypass
    - **Track Sends** allows linking volume, mute, pan, and LFE (Low Frequency Effects) settings
    - **Mix** attributes allows linking Record Enable, Input Monitoring, Solos, and Automation Modes

For now, let's just create an **Edit** group for our entire Drums ID "*D*" and subgroups for my kicks "*K*", snare "*S*", toms "*T*", and overheads "*O*". Now, if my key focus is on the group window, I can just press the *D*, *K*, *S*, *T*, or *O* keys to enable or disable each one of them.

A bit of navigation

Zooming in and out of the project is an essential DAW feature. We can use the standard *R* and *T* keys to zoom in and out, but sometimes they are not enough. Here are a few other options that Pro Tools can offer:

Project overview

To fit the entire project inside the **Edit** window, use the following two shortcuts:

- *command + option + control* + Down arrow (Mac), or *Ctrl + Start + Alt* + Down arrow (Windows) to resize the entire project's track height to a minimum

- *option* + *A* (Mac) or *Alt* + *A* (Windows) will fit the entire project timeline inside the **Edit** window, giving a real quick way of zooming out for a project overview

Zoom presets and zoom toggle

When working with high track counts, it can be beneficial to quickly zoom in and zoom out. Pro Tools offers zoom presets accessible from the main toolbar linked from numbers *1* to *5* above the letter keys. To set a new zoom preset, just hold *command* (Mac) and *Ctrl* (Windows) and click on the zoom preset icon number available in the top-left area of the **Edit** window.

Zoom presets are very handy but limited to zoom on the current selection cursor and not on ranges, so we cannot select the whole chorus and hit *5* to zoom on it. Instead, we have to use two more shortcuts:

- *option* + *A* (Mac) or *Alt* + *A* (Windows), as seen earlier
- *option* + *F* (Mac) or *Alt* + *F* (Windows) will allow you to fit an edit selection to the **Edit** window

Another good method is the **Zoom Toggle** function accessible with the key command *E* when the key command focus is enabled for the **Edit** window. **Zoom Toggle** has its own settings, accessible by navigating to **Preferences | Editing | Zoom Toggle**. The default settings are not very useful to me; use the following settings to configure as described earlier:

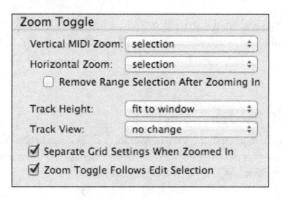

Zoom Toggle preferences

Toggling between zoom presets or zoom toggle will allow for quick zooms inside the project and back to an arrangement overview. As the next screenshot shows, we can zoom in or zoom out a small edit selection at the press of a key.

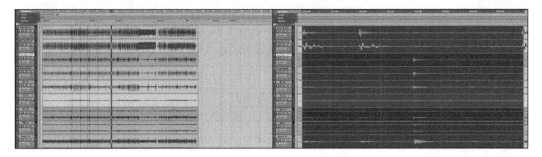

Toggling between arrangement and part focus, zooming on the selected range. The right screenshot is the fit to screen of the left screenshot selection.

Clip groups

Clips groups is Pro Tools way of aggregating clips together for easier editing. It works with audio, MIDI, and video tracks on consecutive or non-adjacent tracks. They become very useful when it comes to moving around chunks of edited clips across the timeline and working on both audio and MIDI tracks.

Let's create a clip group on the selected range across all the drum tracks. We can also interact with clip groups with the following key commands:

	Mac	Windows
Group	*command + option + G*	*Ctrl + Alt + G*
Ungroup	*command + option + U*	*Ctrl + Alt + U*
Regroup	*command + option + R*	*Ctrl + Alt + R*

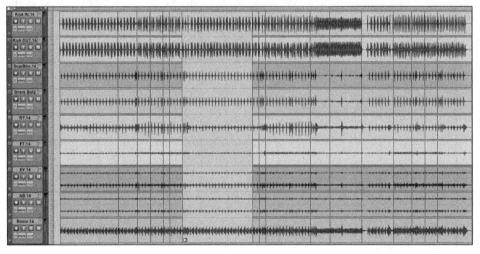

Clip group is shown in the middle

Before moving anything across the timeline, if we have created automation already, let's not forget to enable the **Automation Follow Edit** option to copy our automations with the clip group. We can access it by navigating to **Option | Automations Follows Edit** or the toolbar icon.

Automation Follow Edit toolbar icon

Clip group is non-destructive, meaning that all the edits, clip gains, and fades are preserved and the clip group can be dissolved for further editing with the delete group function. We cannot delete a part of a clip group and would have to dissolve the entire clip every time, or separate the clip group and then dissolve it.

Moving clip groups around follows the same logic as any other normal clip. We can use all the regular copy, paste, and cut shortcuts as well as key modifiers. They can also be faded and processed with AudioSuite, but with this latest option, we would not be able to revert it except with the undo function, as Pro Tools will create new audio files and replace the file.

Selection techniques

There are many ways to make selections in Pro Tools, and also a few shortcuts to improve workflow:

Tab to Transient or Tab to clip edges

Depending on whether the **Tab to Transient** option is enabled or not, pressing the *Tab* key (with or without modifiers) will either jump to the next transient or to the next clip edge.

Tab to Transient icon

Here are the Tab to Transient shortcuts:

	Mac	Windows
Go to next transient	*tab*	*Tab*
Go to previous transient/clip edge	*option + tab*	*Alt + Tab*
Extend selection to the next transient/clip edge	*shift + tab*	*Shift + Tab*

	Mac	Windows
Extend selection to the previous transient/clip edge	*option + shift + tab*	*Alt + Shift + Tab*
Toggle Tab to Transient ON or OFF	*command + option + tab*	*Ctrl + Alt + Tab*
Select to previous transient	*option + shift + tab*	*Alt + Shift + Tab*

Enable Tab to Transient with a grouped track, this will help you to cut your drum performance manually very fast and also avoid false triggers when using Beat Detective to automate the process instead. We will see what Beat Detective can do for us later in this chapter.

Disable Tab to Transient to jump to the next clip edge. This is very useful when editing a batch of fades.

Other selection techniques

If we modified our selection to the previous or next transient, we might want to fine tune the edit to avoid clicks. We can easily do it using the nudge value key commands after setting the appropriate nudge units and values; I usually set this to 1 ms.

	Mac	Windows
Extend/trim selection beginning	*option + shift +* + or - on numeric keypad	*Alt + Shift +* + or - on numeric keypad
Extend/trim selection end	*command + shift +* + or - on numeric keypad	*Ctrl + Shift +* + or - on numeric keypad

 If we were working with an already edited audio and would like to select a range, we can use the / key to make a timeline selection, assuming that the **Link Timeline and Edit selection** option is enabled. For example, if my main counter is set to Bar/Beat and I would like to select bar 9 to bar 28, I can type the following using the numeric keypad: /9/28.

The following shortcut keys can be used:

- To separate (splice) an edit selection, press *command + E* (Mac) or *Ctrl + E* (Windows) or *B* with the **Edit** window key focus enabled. We can then copy or cut it using the regular key commands.

- To move the selection by the nudge value, press the + and - keys on the numeric keypad.

- To move the content within the clip, hold *control* (Mac) or Start (Windows) and the + or – keys on the numeric keypad.

Beat Detective

As we saw previously, Beat Detective is a powerful tool for analyzing rhythmic performances and extracting groove templates. When it comes to correct drum performances, we can use Beat Detective to perform many other tasks. The standard Beat Detective procedure has four steps:

1. **Bar/Beat Marker Generation**: This is used to analyze and create bar/beat markers on which the next steps will be based:

    1. Make an edit selection.

    2. In the **Selection** section, press **Capture**.

    3. In the **Detection** window, click on **Analyze** and adjust the **Sensitivity** slider to match or be as close as possible to your previously selected resolution settings.

2. **Clip Separation**: This section allows for separating the clips on the generated Bar/Beats markers. If there is nothing to adjust, click on **Separate.**

3. **Clip Conform**: Much like the **Quantize** window, it performs quantization and groove functions to match the separated clips to the grid. The **Standard** tab will quantize to the grid and let you apply some swing too. The **Groove** tab lets you apply any user-made groove templates or factory ones.

4. **Edit smoothing**: This is a batch fade smoothing tool, used to fill and crossfade the gaps created by the clip conform function. Click on **Smooth**. Adjust the crossfade settings to your liking, but 5 to 10 ms is a good start for drums.

These four steps will be used in both **Normal** and **Collection** modes, which refer to the two different methods of analyzing audio with Beat Detective's **Bar/Beat Marker Generation** process.

Normal mode

In step 1 of the Beat Detective procedure, we analyzed the audio (or MIDI) clip to create bar/beat markers. When working on a single track, this will be fine. However, if we are trying to cut a drum multitrack all at once, we have to select multiple clips together.

With the normal mode, Beat Detective will generate markers based on the combined transients of all the selected tracks. Many problems arise with this technique, especially when working with the recorded drums; adjusting the sensitivity fader usually ends up with too many or too few markers.

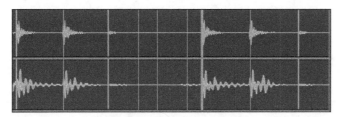

Beat Detective false markers

We can manually add a marker by clicking on the clip with the grabber tool, or remove it by holding *option* (Mac) or *Alt* (Windows) and clicking on the marker. This method can be a bit time consuming.

When a drummer plays to the click and his or her hits are far behind or far ahead, beat triggers, which follow the recorded audio, can be assigned to the wrong bar divisions. To make sure every Bar/Beat marker is linking to the correct grid position, we can display the information on the clip next to the markers by clicking on the **Show Trigger Time** box. If any of them is wrong, we can correct this by double-clicking on the marker and enter the correct Bar/Beat value. The window is the same as the Identify Beat function we will see later.

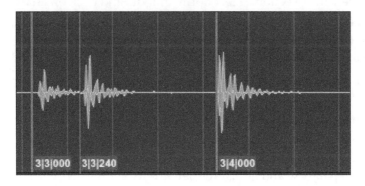

Trigger time displayed

 One good way of working in the normal mode and avoiding too many wrong triggers is to divide your song into sections and work on them one at a time, because different type of playing can lead to different time signatures and velocity, fooling Beat Detective.

Collection mode

Collection mode is a more advanced way of collecting information to generate Bar/Beat markers. This mode allows adjusting the detection settings for each track individually (kick, snare, hi-hat, or any other of your choice) and then copy the combined result across other tracks.

For example, we can analyze kick and then snare, collect both the information, and separate the other microphones following the bar/beat markers generated by kick and snare only. When using collection mode, it is also preferable to use the closest microphones, as sound takes time to travel and triggering from microphones further away will cut the closer ones when it comes to separating the clips. By working with the closest ones, we ensure that we keep all the information.

To use collection mode, from step 1 of the Beat Detective procedure, select **Collection** from the **Selection** drop-down menu inside the **Beat Detective** window.

- **Add All**: This clears collection and adds current triggers
- **Add Unique**: This adds current triggers to the existing collection
- **Clear all**: This clear all triggers from the collection

The trick is to alternate between the collection mode and the normal mode for step 1 of the Beat Detective procedure, then move to the next step. To collect bar/beat markers, perform the following steps:

1. Capture your selection, select normal mode, and click on **analyze**.

2. Adjust the **sensitivity** settings, edit markers manually if necessary, then select **Collection** from the **Detection** drop-down menu and press **Add All** to save them to the collection; lets call it "memory".

3. Select the **normal** mode instead of the collection mode.

4. Now the first track is collected. Let's move the selection to the next track, to add to the collection memory. Keep the exact same edit-selection position with the key command ; to move the selection down, or *P* to move the selection up.

5. Click on **Analyze** and adjust the **sensitivity** settings. You can also edit the markers, if necessary.

6. Switch back to collection mode and click on **Add Unique** to ask Pro Tools to try to figure out if two hits are very close to each other. If they are, they should be considered as one and the latest one should be discarded, or click on **Add All** to add every trigger regardless of the position.

7. If you need to add more tracks, repeat from step 3 of this procedure.

8. Now that we have collected the correct Bar/Beats markers in the memory, the only thing we have to do is to extend the selection of all the tracks using the *;* and *P* shortcuts, but press *Shift* to make a selection, that is, *Shift + ;* or *Shift + P*.

9. Move to the **Clip Separation** tab and continue to correct and quantize the drum performance or use the **Groove Template Extraction** function to save this groove before editing it.

 Groove templates using multiple collections across many instruments in the track can lead to very interesting Band Grooves.

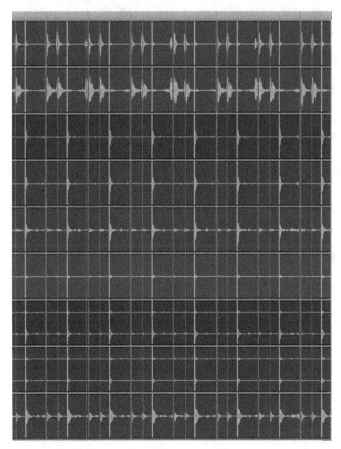

All tracks selected following the kick and snare generated bar/beats markers

Don't forget to use the **Clear All** function of the collection mode window before working on other sections of the song.

Mapping project tempo to the audio

Tempo mapping is the opposite of quantizing. No drummer is a perfect drum machine; they can sometimes be too off tempo, but on the other hand, programming or quantizing drums on perfect grid timing usually ends up with clinical and lifeless performances. The tiny variations in tempo that each player bring to the table shows us that tempo is not always 100% steady, and this can be a good thing. Instead of adding artificial grooves or user-made groove templates, we could create a tempo map of the performance to automate tempo changes, matching the recorded performance.

Using Identify Beat

The simplest and safest way of mapping tempo is to use the **Identify Beat** function pressing *command + I* (Mac) or *Ctrl + I* (Windows), beginning from the first beat and working our way to the end, identifying every bars/beat, and/or finer divisions. This is time consuming, but usually never goes wrong.

Using Beat Detective

I usually do create tempo maps on beat divisions in the collection modes, using the generate **Bar | Beat Generation** function. This feature allows for converting the bar/beat markers into tempo change events, creating a tempo map.

In the **Beat Detective** window, preferably using the collection mode, create a Bar/Beat marker with the **Beats** resolution. Why not sub-Beats? Using finer beats subdivisions can often lead to too many tempo changes and also many manual adjustments.

Sticking to **Beats** and analyzing the kick and snare using the collection mode works really well; I find myself creating perfect tempo maps in less than 10 minutes. On complex rhythmic patterns and song structures, this method works even better when analyzing one part of the song at a time (verse, chorus, middle eight, and so on). When we have correctly analyzed and created our bar/beat markers, click on the **Generate** button at the bottom of the Beat Detective's **Bar/Beat Marker Generation** window.

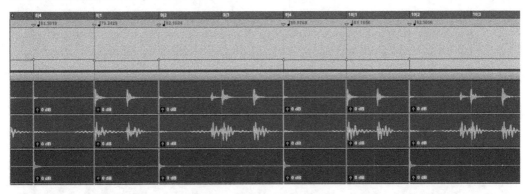

Tempo map created. Notice the tempo changes and that the grid now matches the drum performance.

If one of your markers was not correctly set and a wrong tempo change was generated, we can revert back with undo or manually modify the wrong tempo events.

To do so, just click on the tempo marker to display the **Identify Beat** window.

To make sure we do not have to manually re-adjust, it is better to display the trigger times and check their position before generating the tempo markers.

Elastic Audio for drums

We saw earlier how to use Elastic Audio on single vocal tracks. Using Elastic Audio on multitrack performances, such as drums is also possible and very powerful. Keep that in mind, because as Elastic Audio relies on time stretching plugins, they will have a very small but sometimes noticeable effect on the sound quality, except for Varispeed. To use Elastic Audio across a drum recording, we can perform the following steps:

1. Create an **Edit** or **Edit/Mix** group of the drum tracks.

2. Make an edit selection, including all your clips.

3. Select **Rhythmic** from the Elastic Audio plugin selector.

4. Select the **Analysis** view, then display the **Elastic Properties** window by using *option + 5* on the numeric keypad (Mac) or *Alt + 5* on the numeric keypad (Windows).

5. Adjust the event sensitivity factor to get a closer match to what you need.

6. Now, manually correct the analysis to get the best out of Elastic Audio. Using the pencil tool, click on any existing marker to promote it across all the tracks (retaining phase coherence). Many of them will already be in the correct place, but many others will need adjustment. We can choose to leave single markers behind; however, if activated, these can degrade the audio quality, as different time-stretching factors might happen across the tracks. Delete individual or grouped markers by holding *option* (Mac) or *Alt* (Windows) and clicking on the marker.

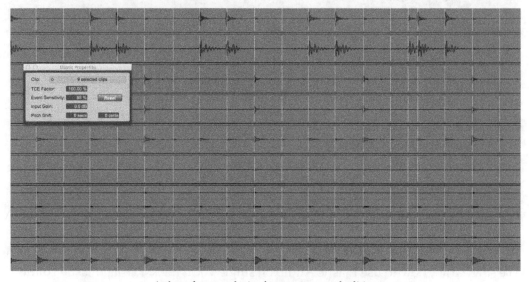

A clean drum analysis after some manual editing

7. Select the **Warp** view and move each hit individually, holding the *Shift* key.

8. Now that our hits are correctly detected, we can conform them to the grid using the **Quantize** window. Select **Elastic Audio Events** and quantize the audio like any other MIDI performance. We can also apply any groove templates we like.

9. Once the performance is tidy, display the **Rhythmic** plugin option window to tweak the decay rate. This setting can be adjusted per track and clip from the **Elastic Properties** window.

 We can do a few more things with Elastic Audio, such as changing the pitch of any clip and changing its overall length with the TCE setting.

Elastic Audio as an effect

Abusing Elastic Audio can create time stretching effects on any kind of material, making it very interesting for sound design. Elastic Audio can perform very astonishing time compressions and expansions. If the plugin operates within its limit, everything should sound ok; however, if we exceed those, the warp display will show red-colored clips. This can result in very interesting sounds, great for sound design.

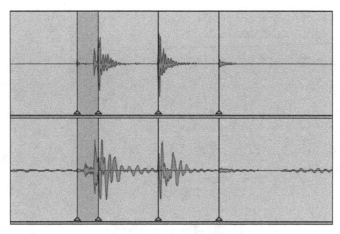

Outside Elastic Audio limits

The vinyl stopping effect using Elastic Audio

The effect of stopping a vinyl is a direct relation between playback speed and pitch. As the playback speed drops, the pitch lowers. To recreate this in Pro Tools, we must first convert our Elastic Audio enabled tracks from **Samples** to **Ticks**.

The **Ticks** setting tells Pro Tools to stretch the content of the track to keep it at the same relative grid position. So if we decrease the tempo, the playback speed will become slower and the audio (or MIDI) events will be stretched accordingly; keeping the track to **Samples** would snap the beginning of the clip to the grid instead.

The other thing we have to do is to change the Elastic Audio plugin to Varispeed, because it is the only plugin that does not keep a consistent pitch while stretching the audio, all the other plugins do. On the other hand, Varispeed does not rely on any time-stretching processing, keeping the full audio quality.

Now we can create a tempo automation to simulate the vinyl effect. Drastic changes can be very interesting and creative.

To create a classic sounding stopping effect, first select a timeline range and display the **Tempo Operations** window:

- *option + 2* on the numeric keypad (Mac)
- *Alt + 2* on the numeric keypad (Windows)

I normally use the parabolic shape, but I encourage experimenting. We can also use the pencil tool to draw odd shapes.

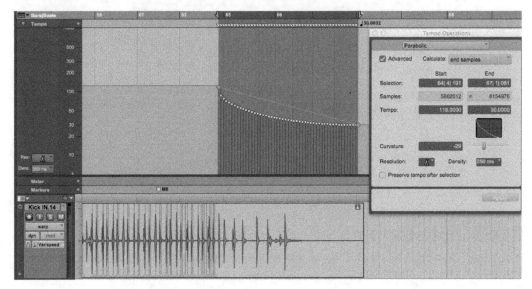

Tempo Automation and Tempo Operations window

Using Vari-Fi

Pro Tools features an AudioSuite plugin called Vari-Fi to quickly and easily get a vinyl-stopping effect. While this effect works quite well across many situations, it does not give any curve control and will therefore always sound similar.

We can find the plugin by navigating to **AudioSuite | Pitch-Shift | Vari-Fi**. To use Vari-Fi:

1. Make an edit selection across one or multiple tracks.
2. Choose **Slow Down** or **Speed Up**.

3. Selecting **Fit To** will constrain the result inside the current selection (handy to do, in the middle of a song) or **Extend** to extend the audio to fit the result (better for a song ending).

4. Fades will either create a fade-in effect if we are speeding up, or a fade-out effect if we are slowing down.

Summary

In this chapter, we saw some important editing techniques and other organizational concepts. Pro Tools is very powerful when it comes to editing an audio. We should try to use shortcuts as much as possible to improve our workflow. Beat Detective and Elastic Audio are two major features that made Pro Tools the industry leader. Mastering those tools will enhance your creativity and speed.

In the next chapter, we will look at some more advanced mixing concepts using hardware inserts, submixes, and automations, to get more out of our mixes in Pro Tools.

3
Advanced Mixing

In this chapter, we will look at some workflow and routing concepts to take full advantage of Pro Tools's mixing capabilities, integrating both hardware analog units with our favorite plugins. Pro Tools offers advanced routing capabilities combined with advanced automation modes for this digital audio age.

Getting organized with colors

You might think that coloring is a side skill and that you can do without it. Many of us still rely on Pro Tools's default track coloring and manually assign their preferred colors to tracks and clips, but there are simpler ways of organizing our visual references.

Let's begin with the default track color coding. Navigate to **Preferences** | **Display** | **Color Coding**. Here you can choose the default coloring scheme for both tracks and clips. By assigning the default track color coding to **Groups**, every time we group tracks together, Pro Tools will automatically assign them to the same available color. By assigning the default clip color coding to track **Color**, we also avoid having a different color for clips and tracks.

This can help busy internal projects where quick organization is essential. While mixing, many tracks often complement each other to create a single melody or sound. Musicians tend to use many harmonies and create multiple different parts, sometimes with different instruments to support or enrich the original melody.

Working on those kinds of projects usually requires many tracks, and grouping them together is essential in order to keep a better track of the arrangement.

Having previously assigned our tracks and clips to some more manageable color coding, it would be nice to display those colors inside the mixer window as well. To do so, we need to adjust the saturation settings from the color palette (**Window** | **Color Palette**) or double-click on the track header in both mix and edit windows.

We can also color the marker ruler with the color palette:

1. Go to **Preferences | Display | Color Coding** and enable the **Always Display Marker Colors** option.

2. Create a marker.

3. Click on it and select its color from the color palette.

While color coding can sometimes seem time consuming at first, it will help us improve our overall workflow as follows:

- Creating a better understanding of the project's structure
- Navigating faster using shortcuts
- Creating custom visual groups

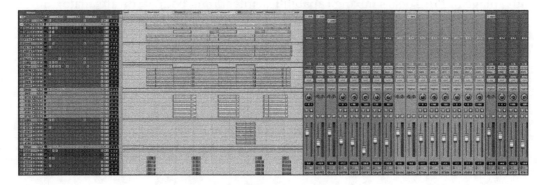

An example of organized color coding for mixing

Inserting analog hardware into the mix

Using hardware units inside the Pro Tools mixer is a great way of bringing some analog sound to your mix. There is quite a lot of confusion regarding the use of hardware units inside the Pro Tools mixer. How do we keep everything in time?

First, to create hardware inserts, navigate to **Preferences | I/O | Insert**. From the **Insert** window, we can create new virtual inserts. You might notice that we have no differentiation between inputs and outputs; this is because an insert will always have the same corresponding I/O. For example, creating a new mono insert on channel 8 will require patching on input 8 and output 8 of my interface.

Now that we have created the insert, there are two possible cases.

We have an Avid interface alongside our HDX, HD Native, or HD Accel cards. In this instance, we have nothing to worry about. Pro Tools will automatically compensate for any hardware delay induced by the A/D and D/A converters. The only time where we might have to manually adjust the delay is when we are using external digital devices such as devices inducing delays or even another **Digital audio workstation (DAW)**. This is because digital units take time to process the signal, resulting in an extra-added delay.

If we are running any configuration other than the Avid HD hardware using Core Audio or ASIO interfaces, Pro Tools will not compensate for any external hardware. We will have to measure and compensate for the A/D and D/A conversion every time.

 If you would like to assign different inputs and outputs, you will need to manually route the signal to external outputs using track sends or track outputs, and record the signal returned using a separate audio track with the correct audio input.

Measuring hardware insert latency

In order to measure the latency induced by the converter, we need a very short transient signal such as a click track.

1. Create a click track and record it as a new audio file Audio1.
2. Create a hardware insert in **Audio1**.
3. Connect the interface output to the matching input according to what we set up previously in **I/O**.
4. Create a new track named Recording, and select the same input number as the one used for the insert.
5. Record the click from **Audio1** onto **Recording**.

6.   To measure the delay, make an edit selection between the original track 1 click position and track 2 click position, and display the main counter in **Min:Secs** to measure the length selection. We can make the selection process easier by grouping both the tracks and using the *Tab* key with or without tab to transient enabled, depending on whether the clip was trimmed or not. I would advice to trim the clip manually and use the *Tab* key without tab to transient. This method can be more accurate since tab to transient can lock the wrong transient.

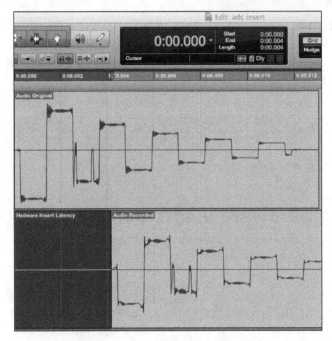

Delay measurement selection and reading

7.   Navigate to **Preferences | I/O | H/W Insert Delay** and enter the corresponding value in milliseconds.

To make sure that this is working correctly, record on track 2 again and check whether your click is on time. You should see this:

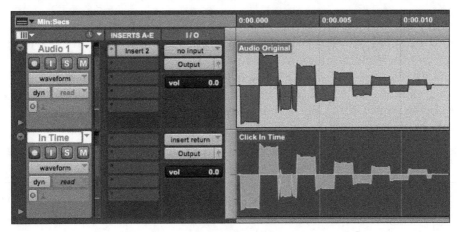

Click on time if ADC works correctly

I would recommend updating your measurements every time you want to use an external unit. Latencies will vary depending on the project's settings. Be very cautious while using hardware inserts.

Because the default manual hardware insert delay compensation from I/O Setup is in milliseconds and not sample accurate, we could also choose not to use it. This will provide us with the latency measurement in samples instead of using the **+/-** user offset delay from the delay compensation track display; alternatively, if we need more than 16,383 samples, we would have to disable ADC for this track entirely and nudge the clips instead.

To stop a track, report its delay to the Delay Compensation engine inside the mix window's delay compensation track display. This can be done by holding the *control + command* (Mac) or *Ctrl* + Start (Windows) keys. Click on the **Dly** line so it is displayed in gray instead of green.

Using hardware sends across different I/O

Hardware sends follow the same rules as hardware inserts. We should measure their latency too, but we cannot compensate for it automatically like we did while using hardware sends on the same I/O. To compensate for processing made across different I/Os, we will have to measure the delay as in the previous section, and put the recorded audio back in time using one of the following options:

- Nudging the audio clip
- Inputting a negative user-offset delay into the delay compensation track settings

Nudging

Nudging is a very important part of the Pro Tools workflow. We can use it to move clips around the timeline and make up for the delay we forgot to compensate beforehand or even create artificial delays to adjust the timing manually. Nudge settings are found in the **Nudge** section of the toolbar. It can be of all unit types and values. Using + and – from the numeric keypad is a must for precise adjustments and can also be used with the following modifiers:

Modifier function	Mac	Windows
Change the nudge value by increment settings (numeric keypad)	*command* + *option* + + or *command* + *option* + –	*Ctrl* + *Alt* + + or *Ctrl* + *Alt* + –
Nudge with the alpha keyboard	*control* + < or *control* + >	Start + < or Start + >
Nudge with the numeric keypad	+ or -	+ or -

We can also enter precise values by clicking on the nudge indicator; this is handy to recover uncompensated delays. To make up for the hardware insert, take the measurement as we saw previously and enter the precise value in samples.

 Alternatively, we can use the **Shift Clip** function from **Edit | Shift** to shift or nudge any edit selection by a precise value. The shortcut for this is *option + H* (Mac) or *Alt + F* (Windows).

Routing and grouping techniques

Managing complex mixes becomes a lot easier when we group our tracks. Pro Tools uses internal buses to route audio inside the mixer. We can use grouping for several reasons such as processing many tracks together or creating stems. We can also group in a parallel way, creating a wet signal that will be mixed back with the dry one. Grouping can be made easier and also more complex to have more control over the mix.

Easy audio grouping

Pro Tools offers an interesting shortcut to assist the process. To create a new audio group, the simplest way is to follow these steps:

1. Select the tracks to be grouped.

2. Press *option + shift* (Mac) or *Alt + Shift* (Windows) and click on the track output.

3. Select **New Track** and create a mono or stereo auxiliary track. The bus name and routing will be automatically assigned.

We can later select or show the corresponding tracks associated with any type of input or output by right-clicking on any track input or output. This also works for hardware sends.

Multiple track outputs

In Pro Tools, a track can have as many outputs as you like (as long as you have available voices); it can even be routed to all available outputs simultaneously. Hold the *control* key (Mac) or Start key (Windows) and click on the track's output to add another output. When a track is routed to multiple outputs, a **+** button is displayed like this:

Routing to multiple outputs; this track is assigned to Mixbus and other outputs

There are also key modifiers that we can use.

Key modifier	Mac	Windows
Add the desired output to all the tracks	*control + option*	Start + *Alt*
Add the desired output to the selected tracks	*control + option + shift*	Start + *Alt + Shift*

Stemming with multiple outputs

Unfortunately, there is no easy way of creating stems or multitrack bounces automatically with Pro Tools 10; the process remains mainly manual. Pro Tools 11 addresses some of these issues in the next section, but for now, assuming that our master fader track contains processing, our first and only stemming option is to solo the appropriate tracks and use the **bounce to disk** function.

If we have no processing for our master output fader, we can bounce inside the session instead by assigning multiple outputs to tracks or buses by grouping them and creating auxiliary sends. Using the key modifiers defined previously, you can quickly select tracks and assign their outputs or auxiliary sends to new audio tracks for recording. To stem tracks to a new audio track without affecting their current routing, use the following methods.

Using multiple outputs

1. Select the tracks.
2. Hold *control* + *option* + *shift* (Mac) or Start + *Alt* + *Shift* (Windows).
3. Click on **New track** from the track output menu.
4. Create the appropriate audio track and record.

Using auxiliary sends

1. Select the tracks.
2. Hold *option* + *shift* (Mac) or *Alt* + *Shift* (Windows).
3. Click on **New track** from the track output menu.
4. Create the appropriate audio track and record.

 We can select the desired recording format from the session window accessible from **Setup | Session**. If you're recording the track at anything other than a 32-bit float, make sure your levels do not exceed 0 dBfs.

We can also use complex mixing routing techniques to our advantage, as this will give us many summing points from which we can easily create the **New track** stems. We will discuss more on how to increase routing complexity to create more summing points inside the mix.

Sound layering

Using auxiliary tracks is the best way to perform parallel processing in Pro Tools, but multiple output routing can also be very useful for sound layering, keeping your track sends free for other effects. By sending the output to multiple auxiliary tracks, we can very easily add textures and effects. As an example, I like to layer my basses this way with different distortions and other parallel processing. To me, sound layering is more suited to multiple outputs because their relative level mostly stays the same.

Stemming with Pro Tools 11

Pro Tools 11 brings new offline bouncing capabilities with added simultaneous bounce from internal busses or physical outputs. Inside the **Bounce to disk** window, click on the + button to add another source to a maximum of 16. Each source can have a different file format, from mono to multichannel audio.

Because we can bounce physical outputs, Pro Tools 11 also allows for stemming tracks that are processed using master fader inserts. These new features added to offline bounces have drastically improved the Pro Tools 10 workflow, saving us a lot of time and leaving us with the following two main stemming options:

- While working with multiple outputs, we can source our stem from the physical outputs directly
- While summing inside Pro Tools, it becomes a lot more relevant to group as many tracks as we can to create available bounce sources

Increasing mixing complexity

One of the biggest advantages of mixing inside a DAW over traditional analogue console setups is its expanded routing capabilities, giving us far more control over the signal. In this section, I'd like to discuss how to use buses to create more complex mixes, that is, creating extra summing points for several uses and comparing the digital approach over a traditional frontend analog mixing console setup.

As we saw previously, Pro Tools 10 introduced a new 64-bit floating point mixer, allowing for almost unlimited headroom and greater precision, which made digital summing even more digitally perfect. This means that it is entirely up to the engineer to create his sound textures through recording or digital processing. Pro Tools 11 took this quest for digital perfection even further with a full 64-bit path.

On the other hand, analog is technically flawed and has always been; every single piece of circuitry will color the signal in various amounts, but these are those imperfections that many of us came to love and successfully or not tried to recreate in the digital domain. A digital mixer will sum signals with a far lower harmonic distortion. Applying different distortions is therefore the key to restore an analog feel to the mix. The first step toward this approach is to increase the mixer's complexity to be able to apply different types of distortions in many more places.

Audio groups or buses are the most basic routing idea. As an example, working with drums, I would group all the kicks together, the snare together, the toms together, the overheads together, the rooms together, and so on. Those subbuses will then be bused to a master drum bus. This allows us to do the following:

- Process multiple microphones at a time
- Bounce stems more easily later
- Have greater control over my individual drum sounds

To me, routing is the heart of digital mixing and making it as complex as possible begins to open many new creative doors.

But we can go a step further. My drum bus will be first bused to my rhythm bus, then to my instrumental bus, and finally to my mix bus. This introduces more advanced groupings based on other criteria such as rhythm or instrumental. This might not seem very useful at first, but it will make you think about the track in different ways, giving you control at every stages of the mix. Here is an example of what a complex mix would look like:

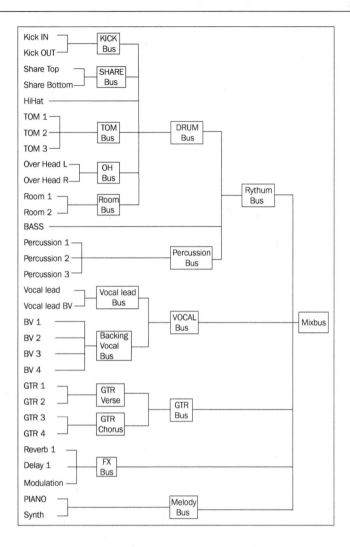

An example of a more complex routing diagram

I might not use all the possibilities all the time, and this is only a small example. But this helped me very much over the years to create better depth in my mixes and also considerably speed up my workflow while creating stem mixes. I have instant access to many more summing points in my mixes, allowing me to group and differentiate even more sounds from each other.

The previous diagram only shows how to increase a mix complexity by busing tracks into each other, but these summing points are also open doors to some very effective parallel processing that we will learn about later in this chapter.

Default output bus options

While working with multiple buses, it becomes quite hard to systematically remember to update the track output to the user's Mixbus. We can change the default track's Pro Tools's default bus output through **Preferences** | **I/O** | **Output** | **Default Output Bus**.

Along with changing the default bus output, there are a few key modifiers worth remembering to assign tracks to the desired output or the bus.

Key modifier	Mac	Windows
Assign all the tracks to the same I/O	*option*	*Alt*
Assign all the selected tracks to the same I/O	*option + shift*	*Alt + Shift*
Assign all the tracks' I/O incrementally	*command + option*	*Ctrl + Alt*
Assign all the selected tracks' I/O incrementally	*command + option + shift*	*Ctrl + Alt + Shift*

Greater control over parallel processing

Parallel processing is widely used for mixing. It allows adding to the signal while preserving the original content. It usually sounds a lot better to mix this way rather than process everything on groups; drums can particularly benefit from this technique.

The main issue with group processing is that it tends to make everything sound very clinical and lifeless, especially if too much dynamic treatment is applied. Digital dynamic processors especially do not compare well to their analog counterpart when it comes to attenuating levels without taking life out of the recording. For these reasons, I tend to complement my mixes with a lot of parallel processing to increase harmonics, depth, loudness, and focus frequencies rather than cutting or boosting them too much. Parallel processing allows me to get a richer sound.

Creating parallel processing requires extra buses. We can use the track sends, multiple outputs, or duplicate the track to achieve quick results.

As an example, using track sends in pre fader mode, I can quickly create a perfect copy of my signal independent of my main mix level to process and automate creatively.

1. Select the tracks and press *command + G* (Mac) or *Ctrl + G* (Windows) to create a new group.

2. Inside the **Create group** window, disable **Follow Global** and select **Mix** or **Edit/Mix** and the appropriate send and settings you would like to link. In my example, I will only link **Volume** and **Mute**.

Now that we have created the group, a neat thing to do would be to copy the existing track volume levels to the send. To do so, perform the following steps:

1. Press *command + option + H* (Mac) or *Ctrl + Alt + H* (Windows).

2. The **Copy to Send** window appears. Select the correct destination send and the parameter to copy. We can copy everything, even automation, to have the exact same mix across the entire song.

3. Now with the tracks still selected, display any send window, hold *option + shift* (Mac) or *Alt + Shift* (Windows), and click on **PRE** to make the sends pre fader and have the auxiliary mix independent of the main mix.

Having copied the current mix to the send, we can not only use it as a perfect parallel copy, but now we also have the choice to alter the balance between the current mix and the send to better suit the type of parallel processing we will be applying. Trying to improve the low end might not require too much high frequency information, so I might change the balance to pull down the appropriate tracks. On the other hand, trying to improve my high end might benefit from pulling down low frequency content.

[Copying mix to send is also very useful while setting up cue mixes for recording.]

Using the copy to send function is very rewarding while working with parallel processing, but the default mixer's send view does not look very user friendly. Pro Tools offers an alternate way of displaying the send information inside the mixer window. We can focus on a particular send to display mini fader sends and level information. To do so, let's navigate to **View | Sends A-E** or **View | Sends F-J** and select the particular send you would like to display. We can also press *command* + click (Mac) or *Ctrl* + click (Windows) from the left-hand side of the send in the mixer view. We can display a maximum of two sends at a time in Pro Tools 10 and all of them simultaneously in Pro Tools 11, giving a great matrix view for parallel processing or headphone mixes. This new functionality is accessible from **View | Expanded Sends**.

Pro Tools 11 Expanded Sends view, showing Sends A-E

We now have a nice send display with linked parameters:

- To change the level of all the grouped tracks, keeping their relative level with the group active, just move one of the send fader

- To change one send value without affecting the entire group, hold *control* (Mac) or Start (Windows) and move the appropriate fader

Advanced side chain

Side chaining is one of the most commonly used techniques for music production, sound design, and mixing. Pro Tools allow for some interesting side chaining possibilities, allowing us to not only mix many different tracks and process them, but also to play with their timing by manipulating the automatic delay compensation.

For bass

I will stay with my drum recording and take the classic example of compressing the bass track according to the kick. By doing so, we make the groove tighter, reinforcing the impression that the bass player is locked to the drum groove. To do so, I could use the Bomb Factory BF76 plugin on the bass with my side chain activated on bus 15 carrying the kick.

Once it is set up, every time the kick hits, the bass track gain will be pulled down, enhancing the groove and also giving more space in the mix for the "kick drum," but that is not all. Since Pro Tools uses buses to create external side chains, we can send as many signals as we'd like to control the bass accordingly.

As an example, I could have the kick not only during the verses but could also add some of my percussion to the side chain mix. Tweaking the side chain balance mix can give you very natural results and give the impression that the bass player is grooving more with the entire performance.

When we group multiple signals together into a side chain, we can also alter their frequency spectrum or even their dynamics to create different compression behaviors. Because my side chain information is contained on a bus, I can create a master fader or auxiliary track to process the audio before it reaches my plugin. While working with recorded drums, it might be useful to gate the side chain bus a lot more aggressively, since it cannot be heard. We can also boost one of the low kick frequencies and cut the high end to avoid hats, crashes, and so on triggering unwanted compressions. To do so, we could boost the low frequencies first and then gate the result more aggressively.

For vocals

We could also use this technique to create a more specialized frequency-dependent compressor. This is very useful not only for vocal work like de-essing but also for attenuating unwanted vocal characters such as a blocked nose or even compensating for unwanted proximity effect. This technique is a bit different, since the side chain contains the same signal. There are two ways to set up the side chain processing: either duplicating the track and using it as a side chain source or using an auxiliary send from the original track to a bus controlled by a master fader.

- To create a de-esser, just add an equalizer to the side chain's bus master track and boost between 5,000 and 8,000 Hertz. It also helps to filter the lower end of the spectrum.

- To mask blocked noses, try to boost between 800 and 2,000 Hertz.

- To soften a voice that's sounds too pushed or is "breaking" too much, try to boost between 1,000 and 4,000 Hertz.

- To compensate for the unwanted proximity effect, we can either attenuate below 150 to 250 Hertz with a shelf EQ, or because the proximity effect varies depending on how far the singer is from the microphone, create a frequency-dependent compressor by filtering the high end and gently boosting the low end of the signal. These are only guidelines, and I invite you to try different settings and frequencies.

As you can see, we can manipulate the side chain signal in many ways to make up for many recording issues. If we are working on an electronic production, one more tip I'd like to share is how to make your side chain compression react faster.

For this, we need a fast transient in the side chain input. Using recorded drums always brings up spill, and even sampled sounds usually fail at providing a clean and fast enough transient. We saw earlier that we can process the side chain signal to make it more effective, but what about replacing the audio altogether? We could substitute the real kick with a more suited waveform. Contemporary dance productions use very fast custom-side chains to induce faster or special rhythmic effects. For a cleaner side chain signal, we can replace the kick with a click recording or by drawing a waveform directly. To draw a waveform, we can follow this procedure:

1. Create a new audio track, click on **Record arm,** and record silence.

2. With the Pencil tool, draw a transient.

3. Duplicate the clip on the desired grid division.

If we zoom in the waveform, we can sometimes see that the waveform begins slightly behind the grid. So, it is good practice to check with a high zoom level and move the clip if necessary; we can also cut the waveform to adjust the initial level of the click.

 We should create a click track once and re-use it later by importing it into other sessions. To do so, we will use the import session data in the next chapter.

To make the click track easier to use when imported into other session, trim the clip to finish very shortly after the click, duplicate the clip for the entire session's length, and do not forget to set **Track mode** to **Tick** to follow any change in tempo.

Using a self-made click track is very useful and precise, but we can also experiment with many other audio files and also drum loops or very complex patterns. Side chaining brings many more possibilities to how we mix audio together, adding more complex interaction between frequencies and dynamics. I wish it was even more deeply implemented into our plugins to trigger any parameter, as this a true contemporary production technique workhorse.

Using automatic delay compensation creatively

Pro Tools not only keeps everything sample-accurate using its automatic Delay Compensation engine but also lets us alter its timing per track. Adding a positive or negative track delay can be very good to adjust performances.

Using the user offset delay setting represented by the **+/-** sign in the track's delay compensation display inside the mixer window and by entering a negative offset, we can move the click track back in time. Here is a small, easy-to-remember reference table from which we can easily calculate our own offsets:

Sample rate	1 second	10 milliseconds	1 millisecond
44.1 kHz	44,100 samples	441 samples	44.1 samples
48 kHz	48,000 samples	480 samples	48 samples
88.2 kHz	88,200 samples	882 samples	88.2 samples
96 kHz	96,000 samples	960 samples	96 samples
192 kHz	1,92,000 samples	1920 samples	192 samples

We could also make an edit selection from the start of the bar until the peak of the waveform to measure it in samples and enter the value in the user offset delay.

The Avid Channel Strip plugin

Pro Tools 10 introduced a brand new channel strip plugin directly taken from their new acquisition of Euphonix. The algorithms are based on the Euphonix System 5 console. Along with being a workhorse for any mixing or sound design with many integrated processors, it also provides different routing options to suit almost any situation. The plugin is composed of the following modules:

- Input and output gain control with peak metering and phase inversion
- Six bands' equalizer module with switchable filters and shelving curves
- The expander/gate module
- The compressor limiter module
- A dedicated side chain processing module
- An overview window
- A module routing window

The Avid Channel Strip Center modules – EXP/GATE (top left), COMP/LIMIT (top right), SIDE CHAIN (bottom left), and overview (bottom right)

I am sure that you already know how to use these types of processors, but let's focus on some useful and not so common parameters that can help us get the most out of the channel strip.

- The **EXP/GATE** module provides a **HYST** parameter allowing for setting up a different threshold to close the gate. This prevents hearing a chatter effect when levels fluctuate too much around a single threshold.
- The compressor offers a **DEPTH** parameter allowing us to set maximum amount of gain reduction, avoiding crushing of the signal too much and making the compression a lot more transparent. I never understood why only a few compressors offer this great functionality.

While many compressors offer the choice between soft or hard knee, the Channel Strip plugin offers a user-defined range of values, making it really versatile.

To display a large gain reduction meter instead of input meters, click on the drop-down menu arrow on the top-right part of the input display.

- The side chain module allows for internal processing of the frequency spectrum with a single band equalizer/filter to tailor the dynamic processing response. We can also choose between different side chain sources: internal, external, or linked side chains. The ALL-LINKED function will process all the channels by the loudest trigger across all the channels. This is much like a stereo link function, but the plugin can also handle up to 7.1 multichannel configurations.

  We can also switch between **PEAK** and **AVG** loudness detection to accommodate all types of signals or desired behaviors.

- The overview module provides a great way of quickly setting up the previous three processing modules by displaying all their parameters on a single page.

- The equalizer is a very clean and versatile EQ. It can be set in a few different configurations, depending on how many filters or shelving we need. While working on the display, we can still control the Q setting and gain separately. Clicking and moving a band cutoff frequency will allow to boost and sweep at the same time. Here are two key modifiers:

Function	Shortcut on Mac	Shortcut on Windows
Q control	*control*	Start
Gain only, frequency locked	*shift*	*Shift*

- The last module accessible from the **FX Chain** drop-down menu allows for four different types of routing within the plugin.

We can choose to place the equalizer and/or filters before or after any dynamic processing, or place the output volume before the processing chain.

I really like this new channel strip because it is versatile and sounds transparent as well as saves me some inserts in many cases. The last advantage is that it has no latency and can therefore be monitored during live recordings.

Master faders

Master faders are level checkers with many other uses. Their outputs can be assigned to any internal or physical buses so we can not only meter but also process the signal more accurately. This is very useful when it comes to auxiliary send processing, and they are also very important with the HD Accel system to make sure that we do not clip the 24-bit word.

They also have post fader inserts making them the first choice for pushing into compressor-style mixing and also, in mastering to apply final dithering. Dithering should always be the last of the chain processing because its purpose is to replace bit depth reduction and other processing rounding errors with a shaped lower-level constant noise in order to make lower-level details more audible.

Master faders can also be used to increase the total inserts to 30 by routing a track output into an auxiliary input track via a bus controlled by a master fader track. The following screenshot illustrates the following routing: track's inserts → bus → master fader bus inserts → auxiliary input track inserts.

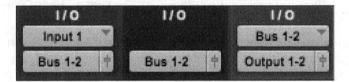

30 inserts routing from left to right – audio track, master fader track, and auxiliary track

Pro Tools and analog console integration

Traditionally, when it comes to multitrack down mixing, Pro Tools was first used to replace a tape machine. We used to record into tape and/or Pro Tools, then output our tracks to discrete channels on the console, added upon the analog bus, and record the console output back onto Pro Tools, tape, or other available mastering recorder. Having a console at the frontend of Pro Tools also helped glue the mix together by adding an analog harmonic distortion to every channel. Working this way is part of the audio engineering heritage because DAWs have come a long way in quality, features, prices, and power, redefining the roles inside modern studio.

Nowadays, we have two main ways of using Pro Tools with our analog console. We could output the tracks to the console's Channel strips to have hands-on mixing experience with the console. Once the mix is done, we usually record the output of the mix bus as the mix and also sometimes record stems or the individual channels separately.

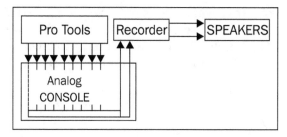

A classic analog mixing signal flow

There are some disadvantages to this approach such as recall. After each mix, the process of writing down all the channel settings, outboard settings, and patching can not only be very tedious but also inaccurate. Recalling an analog mix is always a bit of a gamble. I hear that back in the days, they used to have assistants doing this; unfortunately, only few of the studios and projects can afford this time-consuming work.

We also have the problem of volume automations from Pro Tools. Because the console is placed after DAW, any change in the level will directly affect any analog compression and harmonic distortions happening in the analog domain. We usually spend a lot of time looking for the "sweet spot" setting; it would be great to keep it. To solve this issue, we have to automate the console faders, which is not always available.

Working with a particular studio also restricts mobility. The ability to transfer easily while traveling from one studio to another is a key element to many engineers' and producers' workflow.

By using the console as an insert instead, we have the choice to record all the channels at any time and replace the relevant clips so that we can continue working outside the studio, if necessary. We might lose the console's analog mix bus sound, but as we will see later, we have a lot of available and convincing software alternatives:

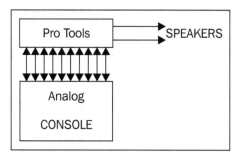

Signal flow using each console's strip as an insert

Let's say my project contains several tracks that I would like to send to my analog console. By using my hardware insert on track insert A followed by a software compressor on track insert B, the signal flow will be as follows: audio clip → console (insert A) → plugin (insert B) → Pro Tools summing mixer → output → speakers.

Now I can record the insert returned from the console onto another audio track, disable insert A, and replace the audio clip with my recording. I could also place my hardware insert at any stage of my mixing environment. In fact, using this technique pushes us to use the console as a bunch of Channel Strip plugins instead. To be as close as possible to the analog mixing environment, we can do any one of the following:

- If we have more virtual tracks than analog strips, we first need to bus our tracks inside Pro Tools, and then place all our hardware inserts on those busses so they fit our console channel count. That way, my buses are processed in the analog domain using hardware inserts, brought back to Pro Tools, and summed up on the 64-bit floating point summing engine. This technique could also be called analog insert stemming.

  After recording our console, we will disable our original tracks and route every recording to the same outputs as their original.

- If we have enough analog strips, we could insert it on every audio track (usually first or last), capturing a lot of analog coloration and sum inside Pro Tools again.

  After recording our console, we will just have to replace the original track clip with the console version. Use playlists to recall easily, if necessary.

- The last option is a combination of any of the two previous scenarios. But it does not really follow any analog logic.

You might think that losing the benefits of a real analog summing is a no-go, and it is for many top engineers and producers, but we can recover the lost analog distortion with some dedicated console emulation plugins that do the job very well. Since Pro Tools 8, Avid brought its own plugin with its **Harmonically Enhanced Algorithm Technology (HEAT)**.

Only available for HDX and HD Accel users, HEAT is a paid option for Pro Tools HD 10 and HD 11 software. Using HEAT, we can add warmth and depth to any mix by creating subtle harmonic distortion on audio tracks only. Unfortunately, HEAT cannot be used on an instrument, auxiliary, or master fader. Other plugin manufacturers have done a really good job at modeling analog consoles' behavior, and we have great recreations from Waves NLS and Slate Digital VCC. Having used all of those three solutions, I can assure that they give great results and push the analog concept a little bit further by allowing us to mix and match many different console styles within a single project and achieve finer results.

As years go by, technological improvements are becoming faster, better, and much more powerful. These technologies, while sounding really good already, are still within their infancy; in my opinion, if not already, they will catch up very soon with real analog hardware. But the best plugins will never be able to replace careful user adjustments and creative changes made possible with automations.

Starting with Pro Tools automations

Automation is one of the biggest advantages of mixing with a DAW. Pro Tools offers a range of automation modes and options and a tight integration with a variety of supported controllers. Using a motorized fader and encoder can be very useful to keep a hands-on experience. I really recommend using a touch-sensitive controller to perform and record automations. Touch sensitivity will allow the software to detect when you touch any of those controllers so tracks can be put in write mode this way.

The track view shortcuts

Toggling between track view selections can be time consuming. Here are a few shortcuts to find the correct automation:

Action	Mac	Windows
Toggle track view for all the tracks	*command* + *option* + *control* + right arrow or *command* + *option* + *control* + right arrow	Ctrl + Alt + Start + left arrow or Ctrl + Alt + Start + right arrow
Toggle track view for a selected track	*command* + *control* + left arrow or *command* + *control* + right arrow	Ctrl + Start + left arrow or Ctrl + Start + right arrow
Toggle the track between waveform and volume	-	-
Toggle all the tracks between waveform and volume	*option* + -	Alt + -

Automation modes

In Pro Tools we can use many automation modes. These can be set and activated separately on each track's header from the track automation mode selector.

- **Read**: No automation is written, only read.

- **Write**: Pro Tools is constantly writing automation on enabled parameters. Regardless of whether they are moved or not, any previous automation will be overwritten. For this reason, by default, Pro Tools will automatically switch to the Touch or Latch mode after each automation passes. We can change this behavior by navigating to **Preferences | Mixing | Automation**.

  - **Touch**: Parameters are written for the time of the automation; it is only then that they are returned to their previous values in a defined timeframe set by the **Automatch** value in **Preferences | Mixing | Automation**. Use the Touch mode to create small automation adjustments as well as sudden automation changes.

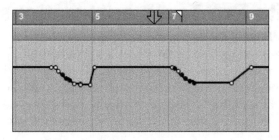

Touch mode examples for fast automatch – bar 5 (200 ms), and slow automatch, bar 9 (1000 ms)

  - **Latch**: This is similar to Touch, but the last value will be kept and written until you stop playback. Latch is the most commonly used automation mode as it allows for a set-and-forget automation procedure. If we stop playback, the automation line will join the previous value with a sudden automation change just like you can see in the preceding example, to the left on the fifth bar. This can be a problem with certain sounds, but we can tweak the automatch transition time to make it less steep.

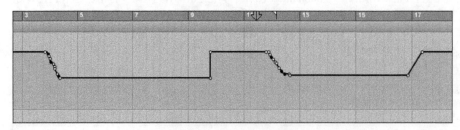

Latch example and automatch

- ° **Touch/Latch**: This mode is a combination of the Touch and Latch modes where the track's volume follows the Touch mode and all the other parameters follow the Latch mode. This can be very useful while adjusting plugins making minor volume adjustments.

- **Trim**: All the volume and volume send automations can be affected by a relative level change set by the Trim automation. A Trim automation can be written with the combination of any other automation mode, for example, Touch Trim, Latch Trim, and Write Trim. Trim adjustments are different from the original volume or volume sends automations and can also be coalesced to original automations for the following uses:

  - ° To display the Trim automation from the track display selector, click on **Volume trim**.

  - ° To coalesce a Trim automation, navigate to **Track | Coalesce trim**.

More automation options

As suggested earlier, we can use side functionalities to complement our automation modes. All of these features are located within the **Automation** window accessible using the keystrokes *command + 4* (Mac), *Ctrl + 4* (Windows), or by navigating to **Window | Automation**. The **Automation** window is divided into sections and allows for suspending all the track automations at the click of the top **Suspend** button.

Enabling the write automation

In the top half, we can globally enable or disable any automation type by just clicking on its icon to display it as red (active) or gray (inactive).

We can also disable automations for a single track only by *command*-clicking (Mac) or *Ctrl*-clicking (Windows) on the automation parameter directly from the track's **Automation** menu. The **Automation** parameter will be grayed out, and this particular automation will be disabled.

Disabling automation is very handy to quickly compare our work with the original and see whether we have made any good improvement, especially while automating vocals.

Manual Write and Write on Stop

When an automation pass is finished or if we have reached the desired value, we can extend the automation value following two sets of **Write to** functions. These actions can be performed while playing (**Manual Write**) or automated to write only after clicking on Stop (**Write on Stop**).

Manual Write options

Manual Write and Write on Stop offer the same set of options: the top row (from left to right) allows us to write the current value to the beginning of the edit selection, the entire selection, or up to the end of the selection. In the following example, I clicked on the write to selection end, and Pro Tools extends the automation to the end of the edit selection.

> While using write to start, end, or all of the selection with no edit selection made, Pro Tools will write the automation to the beginning, end, or the entire length of the project instead respectively.

The bottom row will write the automations to the previous or the next breakpoint as you can see here.

Write on Stop can be good while adjusting parameters; it saves you from having to click on the right button.

We can also mix and match the write to functions by selecting which tracks we would like to apply it to. To mix and match different automation writing, perform the following steps:

1. Automate a few tracks.
2. Before clicking on **Write to**, select some of the automated tracks.
3. Press *option + shift* (Mac) or *Alt + Shift* (Windows), and click on the relevant **Write to** functions.

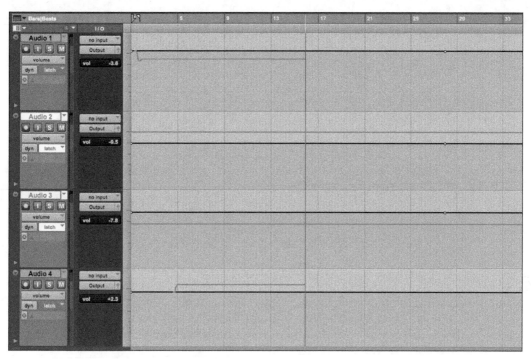

Automated tracks – the selected tracks have been written to the entire project length while still writing automation on others

Auto Join

The **AUTO JOIN** function, accessible from the **Automation** window, is a little gem of the automation workflow as it allows us to stop recording the automation, come back later, and continue writing from the exact same position where we left them. To enable Auto Join, turn the automation mode to latch and click on the **AUTO JOIN** button like this:

Auto Join

We can now begin to record any type of automation and press Stop. In the following example, I will stop recording my volume automation. Pro Tools will display a vertical red line where I stopped recording before the fifth bar as shown in the following screenshot:

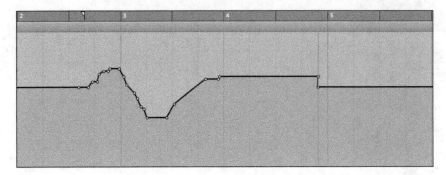

The Auto Join resume line

I can now rewind the playback head and press Stop again. As we are in the Latch mode, the line will be automatically continued with the same value, but I could still choose to begin writing automations before reaching the join line instead.

Trying new mix settings with preview mode

When automations have been written, we cannot change the affected controller value without jumping back or overwriting the previous automation. To prevent this, we can either set the automation selector to **OFF** or temporarily bypass the automation lane as we saw earlier.

Pro Tools offers a solution to this workflow issue with the preview mode. Preview allows us to make parameter adjustments and listen to the results in real time without losing the original automation. To engage the preview mode, perform the following steps:

1. Click on **PREVIEW**.
2. Modify the parameter until you find the correct setting. Once a setting has been changed, the automation mode selector will light up in green to show that preview mode is active on this track.

Preview and Punch in preview

When it comes to writing the current setting, we have a couple of choices:

- Click on punch preview (arrow pointing down at the right of **PREVIEW**) to begin writing automations from the place where you punched in. This function will disable preview at the same time. If you decide to change your mind, undo the last action.

Clicking on punch preview will begin writing to all preview-enabled parameters. If we decide to keep some settings and would like to write only some of the settings, we can use punch capture on selected tracks by pressing *option* + *shift* + click (Mac) or *Alt* + *Shift* (Windows).

- Use the Manual Write or Write on Stop functions to overwrite the previous setting without having to quit the preview mode.

Copying and recalling automations to other song sections

Songs are usually composed of recurring structures, often with similar instrumentation. Let's say that I tweaked all the parameters from my first chorus and would like to copy those settings to the second chorus. The capture mode is there to take a snapshot of the current automation settings so we can insert them again later on. Capture can be used in three ways.

It can be used to capture any currently writing parameters by clicking on the **CAPTURE** button.

1. While writing a parameter, click on **CAPTURE**.
2. Press Stop and move the playback head where you would like to punch in the new settings.
3. Click on punch capture and Press Play.

It can be used to capture an already written automation.

1. Make sure that the track is write-enabled and selected.
2. Press *option* + *shift* (Mac) or *Alt* + *Shift* (Windows) and the **CAPTURE** button to capture.
3. Press *option* + *shift* (Mac) or *Alt* + *Shift* (Windows) and click on the punch capture button.

It can also be used to capture all write-enabled parameters in the session.

1. Make sure that all the tracks are write-enabled.
2. Press *option* (Mac) or *Alt* (Windows) and the **CAPTURE** button to capture.

3. Move the playback head to another location.

4. Press *option* (Mac) or *Alt* (Windows) and the punch capture button.

Capture (left) and punch capture (down arrow to the right)

Preview, capture, and punch are amazing automation options, especially while working on your first mix by sections. While building a mix, we usually create different settings per section and are able to try new ones easily (preview). Capturing those parameters and writing or punching those parameters to other song sections will increase your mixing possibilities.

Glide automations

Glide is an interesting feature to create ramp automation transitions inside an edit selection. Glide automation works as follows:

1. Make an edit selection. The ramp automation will begin from the beginning of the edit selection.

2. Move the parameter you would like to glide to the desired value. In my example, I will move the volume slider to -40 dB.

3. Press *option* + / (Mac) or *Alt* + / (Windows) to create a ramp automation to the desired value.

4. The last value will be carried to the end of the timeline or to the next automation breakpoint.

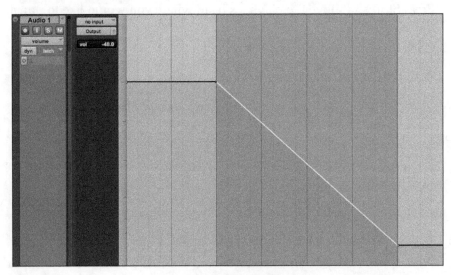

Glide automation created

We can also create glide automations across all the tracks — very nice to create batch fades.

1. Activate the **All** group.
2. Make the edit selection.
3. Move the volume fader to minus infinity.
4. Press *option* + *shift* + / (Mac) or *Alt* + *Shift* + / (Windows).

VCA mixing

VCA tracks are an inheritance of the analog console. Traditionally, VCA groups would allow the engineer to control as many faders as they like with a single VCA group fader, giving him easier control and more choice on his gain stage while grouping audio tracks together to a bus. While VCA used to be assigned to the fader via VCA groups, Pro Tools VCA are assigned to mix groups instead; so to create a VCA, we need to create mix groups first. VCA faders are really handy when creating alternate mixes or fine-tune existing balance.

To create a VCA master, perform the following steps:

1. Create a mix group.
2. Create a VCA master track.
3. Assign the VCA to the mix group from the track's output selector.

When a VCA is created, the slave tracks will always follow the VCA master for the following settings:

* Main volume
* Solo
* Mute
* Input monitoring
* Record

Those controls will be unavailable for individual subgroup linking unless **Standard VCA Logic for Group Attributes** is disabled in **Preferences | Mixing | Automation**.

Why would we use VCA faders instead of conventional audio groups? To explain this better, let's take the following routing example: audio track output → bus 1 → auxiliary track (with compression plugins).

No VCA here, but this example illustrates how we can already control our level on the audio track or on the bus via a master fader or on the auxiliary track's output. So if we have a compressor on our auxiliary track, changing the audio track or master fader track level will change the level at the input of the compressor. Changing the auxiliary track level will not change the compressor's gain reduction.

Creating a VCA group instead of an auxiliary track can add simplicity to the mix. If you do not need to process the group or if you are working without any submixes, sending all your tracks to physical outputs or VCAs can be more convenient; however, Pro Tools VCA also goes beyond their original purpose and becomes even more interesting when assigned to unrelated tracks or a custom set of tracks for different purposes as follows:

- Control multiple sources for "push into the compressor" mixing. We do this by controlling groups of audio tracks bussed into an auxiliary track. It is very useful to increase the loudness.

- Create alternate mixes with a mix group containing all your vocals, and put the VCA at -3 dB for a vocal down mix. Once your vocal down mix is done, you can just disable the VCA to go back to my original mix. In fact, VCA allows you to perform many alternate mixes at the touch of a single fader.

- Facilitates odd automations by creating custom mix group faders. since a VCA can control any combination of tracks, we can easily create complex VCA routings to bring a selection of instruments up or down within parts of the mix.

- Control a particular set of harmonies within a busy arrangement or an instrument character such as room ambience for drums.

VCA masters, such as trim automation, are running alongside any existing volume automations; they can also be coalesced if necessary. To coalesce a VCA automation to its affected tracks, navigate to **Track | Coalesce VCA master automation** or right-click on the track name display.

Pro Tools automation features are diverse and very effective, especially while using Avid controllers with them, but we saw earlier that we can also use some third-party MIDI controllers. Let's have a look at how to create drastic automation changes within the project using Latch Prime.

Use of an MIDI controller with Latch Prime

MIDI controllers using MIDI pots instead of encoders can be tricky to automate in sudden changes. Latch Prime is particularly suited for applications where large numbers of settings have to be automated in one go and especially if they begin with a sudden change in value. Without Latch Prime, changing a parameter value in the stop mode will jump back to the previous state. As soon as you press Play, Latch Prime allows those parameters to be armed for automation recording in the stop mode, keeping the same value when you press Play. I will describe the procedure to use Latch Prime in stop with a MIDI controller and automate a sudden change in the automation parameter.

1. Map your plugin parameters using MIDI learn or plugin mapping with supported hardware by navigating to **Setup | Preferences | Mixing and tick Allow Latch Prime in Stop**.

2. Enable the desired plugin parameters for automation.

3. Move your playback cursor to the section where you would like the change to begin.

4. Enable **Latch automation** on the track.

5. Display the required parameters and adjust them to your liking. Let's say we automate the filter cutoff and resonance of the bass while riding the dry/wet mix of a delay, so we will probably start with the cutoff low and the resonance high and a 100 percent wet delay.

    Now every parameter you have touched (if the hardware supports it) or that you changed will be enabled for automation in the Latch mode, so it will remain at the same position for the duration of the automation.

6. Press Play and adjust the parameters until you reach the desired effect.

7. If you want to start again, just click on undo (*command + Z*) and start from step 6 again.

8. When done, click on stop or use the Auto Join function.

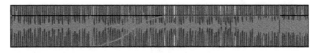

A typical use of Latch Prime in stop; sudden change automated back to its original value

Summary

In this chapter, we saw that Pro Tools really is a world class mixing software. It allows for great, complex mixes while unleashing many creative uses of their functions through automations and grouping. These techniques are the ground for a lot of fun, mixing, and working with the software. I highly recommend understanding all of them in order to create or improve your own workflow.

Now that we have created a mix using analog gear, complex submixes, and automations, let's see how we can share our work by importing, exporting, and working across different projects.

4

Importing and Exporting Options

In the previous chapter we saw some advanced editing and mixing techniques, but it is also very important to keep a tidy project. In this chapter we will see how to optimize our file imports as well as take interactions between different projects further.

Importing audio

Importing audio in Pro Tools is very straightforward, but there are a few options we should look at. The **Import Audio** window is the best way to import audio into your project because it gives a good overview and control of the import process. To open the **Import Audio** window, press *command + shift + I* (Mac) or *Ctrl + Shift + I* (Windows).

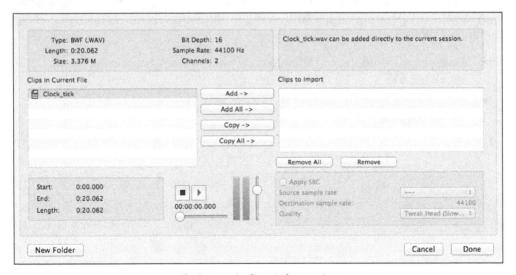

The Import Audio window settings

On the top-left are displayed the file's properties. Selecting a different file from the left list will display its properties at the top.

Since Pro Tools 10, we can use the 32-bit float file format support making it easier to import files from other DAWs. Many of us use more than one DAW and transferring files between them can be tricky, especially if we begin mixing in one and decide to import it later into another. Bouncing files at 32-bit float eliminate the need for dither and checking for channels and master clipping before exporting. We can now just click on **Bounce** regardless of internal levels.

Another novelty is the ability to mix different bit depths within a session. Before this, every file has to be confirmed at the session bit depth. We can now import any file and change the session bit depth at any time to record new files in a new bit depth.

Audio can be added to the session in the following two ways:

- **Add**: This option will simply reference the file on its original drive location without copying it to the project's Audio folder. We can add files at different sample rates, but they will play at the wrong speed.

- **Copy**: This will create a new audio file within the session's audio files folder (by default unless changed with disk allocation, which I will explain later in this chapter). If the sample rate is different than the session's default, this option will change to **Convert; still creating a new audio file. This option is the safest and should always be used to keep the session self-contained.**

We can also drag-and-drop audio files directly from the operating system's browser. While dragging files, the original audio file will be added (not copied) unless its sample rate mismatches with the session and therefore be converted, creating a new file by default. Depending on the section of the edit window, Pro Tools will react differently as follows:

- Drag the file onto the track list to create a new track containing the imported file

- Drag the file onto an existing track lane of the edit window to create a new track clip

- Drag the file onto a blank area of the edit window to open a pop-up dialog with import options

- Drag the file onto the clip list to add the file to the list without creating any new tracks

While dragging files from the operating system browser, the next four options are relevant and accessible from **Preferences | Processing | Import**.

Import

- ☐ Convert Imported ".wav" Files to AES31/Broadcast Wave
- ☐ Automatically Copy Files on Import
- ☐ Convert Copied Files to Session Format
- ☐ Don't convert Sample Rate on Import

Preference import options

- **Convert Imported ".wav" files to AES31/Broadcast Wave**: Select this checkbox to include timestamps in your newly imported WAV files.

- **Automatically Copy Files on Import**: Select this checkbox to make sure every file you drag from the browser will be copied.

- **Convert Copied Files to Session Format**: Select this checkbox to confirm the file format, bit depth, and sample rate to the session file.

- **Don't convert Sample Rate on Import**: By default, Pro Tools will convert every file to match the session's sample rate. Select this checkbox not to match the sample rate but files will playback at the wrong speed and pitch.

Importing session data

Pro Tools can import tracks, settings, and session information from any session file. This feature is not only very powerful for mixing, but also housekeeping and other tricks. To open the **Import Session Data** window, perform the following steps:

1. Use *command + option + shift + I* (Mac) or *Alt + Shift +I* (Windows).

2. Navigate and choose a session file.

The Import Session Data window

From the **Import Session Data** window, we can import any track type track settings, tempo information, time code, window configurations, and more. I use this feature all the time to experiment with new mixes that I saved under different session names. If something goes wrong, I can always bring back any track into my current session to either replace or add. As you can see from the preceding and next screenshots, I have multiple import options but I'd like to focus on two options. First is the replace track option; there are two main ways of replacing or importing track data:

- The automatic way only works if your sessions have the exact same track names. To do so just select the track from the source list and click on **Match Tracks**. Pro Tools will look for similar tracks in your current project and replace settings according to the user-defined options that we will look at later.

- The manual way lets you match the source track with a new track or replace an existing track inside the session. To do so, click on the **Destination:** menu and choose from there.

Importing session data can have the options as shown in the following screenshot:

```
All
None

✓ Alternate PlayLists
✓ Clips and Media
✓ Clip Gain
✓ Volume Automation And Setting
✓ Pan Automation And Setting
✓ Mute Automation And Setting
✓ Main Output Assignments
✓ Send Output Assignments
✓ Plug-In Assignments
✓ Plug-In Settings And Automation
✓ Elastic Audio Track State
✓ HW Insert Assignments
✓ Voice Assignments
✓ Input Assignments
✓ Sidechain Assignments
✓ Track Active State
✓ Track Comments
✓ Track Colors
✓ Record Safe / Solo Safe Settings
✓ Track View Settings
✓ Mix / Edit Groups
  ICON Custom Fader Groups
  ICON Automation Snapshots
```

The destination import option

By default, all the preceding options will be selected, including the main playlist that can be selected from **Main Playlist Options:**. Import track options are very powerful, selecting all and the main playlists will essentially replace everything on the existing track or import it to a new track.

Apart from this reason, we can use the **Import Session Data** window to speed up mixing and also recall our very own effect. It becomes hard to keep track of all the new discoveries and tricks while working on many projects and genres at a time. I tend to re-use some effects with slight variations to fit the current project. Many of them include complex inserts settings and even routings. Importing session data is a great way of keeping track of all these effects over time and recalling them in a few clicks.

Doing so involves the creation of a template session file; in my case, FX templates, where at the end of each mix, I import FX chains that I'd like to keep for later use. Examples of FX templates include the following:

- Click tracks with different sounds and types
- Delays with many tempo variations and types
- Reverbs with different colorations, types, and lengths
- Parallel processing with many different types and purposes
- Spatial effects including delay based and modulation based
- Bus processing for many different applications
- Modulation effects like chorus and filters

I could go on and on as my list is growing every day. I sometimes open this session file to realize how far I have come because I only keep the good ones obviously.

Keeping track of new effect chains can help improve your sound as a mixing engineer, and also helps to reassess some of the techniques that you might have previously used: what works and what doesn't.

We can also use this feature while mixing albums to help get a more cohesive sound overhaul. Hiring a studio for a few days to record an EP or an album usually leads to a very consistent recording sound. While working on a project like this, I tend to begin with the most exciting track and get as far as I can. By the time I finish mixing the first track, I'd already define the sound of the album. Re-using some of the processing is usually very beneficial not only for consistency but also for mix and sound improvement. Here is a little workflow trick that I hope will inspire you to create or improve your own project:

1. Mix the first track. Spend as much time as you can to create a finished mix.
2. Open the second track and begin importing the base track processing, meaning the instruments used across all songs. We can do this by importing plugin chains of the previous mix.
3. Mix the remaining instruments.
4. Go to the third track and improve it from the first two by adjusting the settings.
5. Work your way up to the last track.
6. As you can see, importing track data can be a powerful and surprising tool that will surely find multiple uses in your workflow too.

Creating stems and exporting clips

Creating stems is common practice for many of us when it comes to collaboration, sharing, or even archiving. Having them ready ensures that we can transfer our session between DAW and also manipulate audio more easily when it comes to remixing.

Because Pro Tools 10 only bounces in real time, it is best to bounce only once to save time. To do so we have to bounce internally. Pro Tools 11 allows offline non-real-time bouncing, but this technique can still be applied.

As we saw earlier, we can use multiple output routing and a bit of submixing to create our stems faster. While doing so we can spend a few minutes routing to new audio tracks and record stems all at once.

While bouncing inside the session or in the box, we can choose the audio format or file type, but since Pro Tools 10, we can not only mix and match different bit rates within a session but also choose for 32-bit floating point interleaved audio files. Interleaved means that multichannel audio streams will be contained within one file rather than multiple mono files. To display the current file format, open the session window by navigating to **Setup | Session** or *command* + 2 (numeric keypad) for Mac or *Ctrl* + 2 (numeric keypad) on Windows.

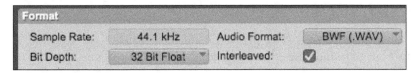

Bit depth selection

 Converting an interleaved file into multiple mono files is lossless and older Pro Tools versions do it automatically on import.

Stems are recorded and we end up with new clips in the edit window with a mix of tracks and stems. To export the stems (or clips) to new audio files, use the export clips as files from the **Clip List** menu or use the shortcuts *command + shift + K* (Mac) or *Ctrl + Shift + K* (Windows). The **Export Selected** window opens as shown in the following screenshot:

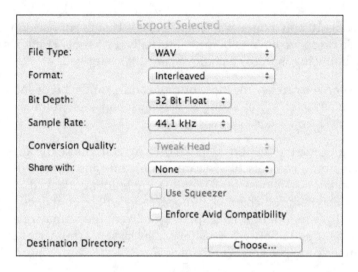

The Export Selected window

Here we can choose the new file's properties. If we recorded our stems at 32-bit floating point, we should select the same to retain full audio quality.

The **Export Selected** window is a really powerful batch export tool allowing for the processing of many clips and converting them to other formats at the same time.

We can also create a stem session in a few clicks. To do so, select the stem tracks and navigate to **File | Export | Export Selected Tracks as New Session**. This will open the **Save Session Copy** window.

Saving a session copy

At the end of a project, we should archive our session using the **Save Session Copy** option. This window has everything we need to aggregate all files and save a new session copy containing all the session tracks, by navigating to **File | Save Copy In**. The **Save Session Copy** window opens as shown in the following screenshot:

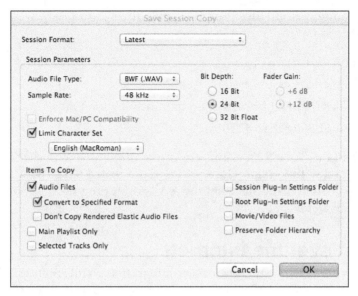

The Save Session Copy window

This window gives a few more options such as sample rate conversion. This is the only way we can convert a Pro Tools session to a different sample rate. While upsampling does not improve the quality of already recorded material, sometimes we can continue recording the project using a higher sample rate.

> While upsampling, I would recommend 88.2 kHz for music purposes and 96 kHz for broadcasting because they are multiples of an integer number of the final sample rate, greatly simplifying the conversion process and therefore, coloring the original recordings a lot less while reducing to 44.1 kHz for music or 48 kHz for broadcast.

Audio Files and **Convert to Specified format** would be automatically checked if we had changed the session sample rate. While keeping the same sample rate, these options are still available to make sure all audio files have the exact same attributes.

We can also convert the session file to open in older Pro Tools versions. Avid continues to support until Version 3.2.

Previous Pro Tools versions

While downgrading session files from Pro Tools 10 or 11 to 7 → 9, we lose the following features:

- Clip gain
- Any 32-bit floating point file format
- Stereo files that will be converted to multiple mono files
- WAV files bigger than 4 GB

Pro Tools 11 and Pro Tools 10 sessions are cross-compatible with the exception of sessions created with Version 11, requiring more than 4 GB of RAM for plugin usage. We also need to make sure that the AAX-64 bit plugins in use have their AAX-32-bit equivalent.

Exporting over the Internet

Pro Tools allows SoundCloud and Gobbler integration. While SoundCloud is very good to showcase our work, Gobbler is geared towards safe cloud backups of our sessions. To sign in to either of those third-party services, navigate to **Setup | Connect to**.

To transfer files to either one of those websites, we can use the bounce to disk functionality and select from the **Share With:** menu.

The Share With: menu

- If we select **Gobbler**, the Gobbler application opens and prompts us with its upload options.
- Using **SoundCloud** opens the following window with all the relevant and even sharing options. This is very handy to share files in a few clicks only:

The Share with SoundCloud window

Missing audio files

Missing files can occur due to many reasons. A warning message will appear while loading the session, presenting us with two search options.

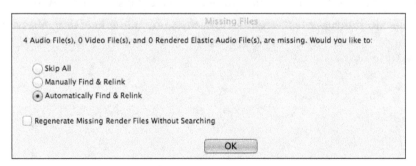

The file missing warning message

Select **Automatically Find & Relink** to scan the entire hard drive according to the original file attributes, including the unique file ID generated for each audio file. This procedure can take a long time and its progress can be monitored in the task manager that we will see a bit later.

While selecting **Manually Find & Relink**, we are presented with the **Relink** window as shown in the following screenshot:

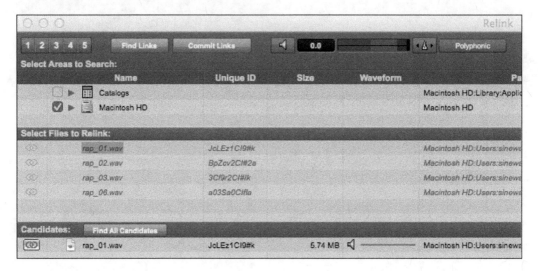

Files relinked

To relink a file, perform the following steps:

1. Browse and select the desired folder or drive; all subfolders will be scanned.

2. Select individual files to relink from the same named section; alternatively, you can also select them all by pressing *command + A* (Mac) or *Ctrl + A* (Windows).

3. Click on **Find Links** and Pro Tools will automatically link the first matching file it finds for each file. Choose the search criteria from the options shown in the following screenshot:

Linking options

4. Select a single file to relink and click on **Find All Candidates** to look for more possible files. This is useful if you keep a permanent backup on the same machine avoiding linking to the backup. New candidates will be displayed in the **Candidates** window.

    A yellow link will appear on each successfully relinked file.

5. Click on **Commit Links** and close the **Relink** window.

6. To view the search indicator progress bar, open the task manager using *option + ;* (Mac) or *Alt + ;* (Windows).

Task manager progress

Disk allocation

Sometimes, conventional hard drives can struggle to keep up with the amount of data. Pro Tools offers the **Disk Allocation** window accessible from the **Setup** menu. This window allows us to allocate different tracks to different hard drives or folders. We can assign tracks manually or automatically using **Round Robin Allocation**. Disk allocation can be very useful to increase the system performance as well as creating custom track folders.

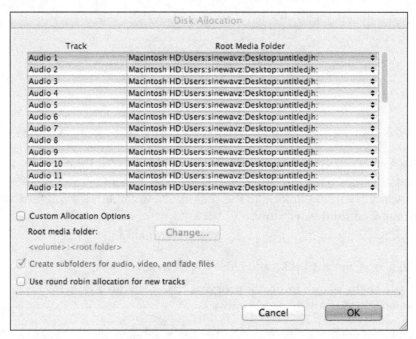

The Disk Allocation window

Pro Tools autobackup

Every computer program can misbehave sometimes and Pro Tools is no exception. Plugins can also add to the issue, causing more incompatibilities and crashes. To make sure we never loose all of our work, Pro Tools offers automatic session files backup that we can configure from **Preferences | Operations**.

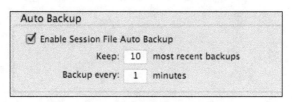

Auto Backup

If a crash occurs, we can manually restore the most recent backup from the `Session File Backups` folder located inside the `Project` folder. We can also revert to the last saved backup by navigating to **File** | **Revert to Saved**.

Summary

In this chapter we saw that basic workflows such as importing media can be done in several ways, each with their advantages and settings. Recovering lost work is also essential to any user in case of a crash. We also saw that any work can be imported into any other project files, therefore, opening many more mixing and setup possibilities. Those functions, even if they can seem secondary to others, should help when it comes to clarifying simple actions where so many things can go wrong, such as missing files or lost work.

Index

Thank you for buying
Pro Tools HD: Advanced Techniques and Workflows

About Packt Publishing

Packt, pronounced 'packed', published its first book "*Mastering phpMyAdmin for Effective MySQL Management*" in April 2004 and subsequently continued to specialize in publishing highly focused books on specific technologies and solutions.

Our books and publications share the experiences of your fellow IT professionals in adapting and customizing today's systems, applications, and frameworks. Our solution based books give you the knowledge and power to customize the software and technologies you're using to get the job done. Packt books are more specific and less general than the IT books you have seen in the past. Our unique business model allows us to bring you more focused information, giving you more of what you need to know, and less of what you don't.

Packt is a modern, yet unique publishing company, which focuses on producing quality, cutting-edge books for communities of developers, administrators, and newbies alike. For more information, please visit our website: www.packtpub.com.

Writing for Packt

We welcome all inquiries from people who are interested in authoring. Book proposals should be sent to author@packtpub.com. If your book idea is still at an early stage and you would like to discuss it first before writing a formal book proposal, contact us; one of our commissioning editors will get in touch with you.

We're not just looking for published authors; if you have strong technical skills but no writing experience, our experienced editors can help you develop a writing career, or simply get some additional reward for your expertise.

Instant Audio Processing with Web Audio

ISBN: 978-1-782168-79-9   Paperback: 76 pages

Learn how to use the Web Audio API to implement audio effects such as loop stitching, audio ducking, and audio equalization through practical, hands-on recipes

1. Learn something new in an Instant! A short, fast, focused guide delivering immediate results

2. Learn Web Audio's scripting abilities by building a broadcast-style audio ducking effect

3. Build a 5-band equalizer using Web Audio's built-in audio processing functionality

Kinect in Motion – Audio and Visual Tracking by Example

ISBN: 978-1-849697-18-7   Paperback: 112 pages

A fast-paced, practical guide including examples, clear instructions, and details for building your own multimodal user interface

1. Step-by-step examples on how to master the essential features of Kinect technology

2. Fully functioning code samples ready to expand and adjust to your need

3. Compact and handy reference on how to adopt a multimodal user interface in your application

Avid Media Composer
6.x Cookbook

ISBN: 978-1-849693-00-4   Paperback: 422 pages

Over 160 highly effective and practical recipes to help beginning and intermediate users get the most from Avid Media Composer 6 editing

1. Hands-on recipes in a step-by-step logical approach to quickly get started with Avid Media Composer and gain deeper understanding

2. Learn Avid Media Composer in a completely new way — gain intensive exposure with various editing options to develop your abilities, become even more creative, and acquaint yourself with various methods that you never thought were possible

LMMS: A Complete Guide
to Dance Music Production:
Beginner's Guide

ISBN: 978-1-849517-04-1   Paperback: 384 pages

The beginner's guide to exploring, understanding, and rocking the world of dance music using the free LMMS digital audio workstation

1. Create the dance music you wanted. An experienced guide shows you the ropes

2. Learn from the best in dance music; its history, its people, and its genres

3. Learn the art of making music: from the way you set up your equipment, to polishing up your final mix

Please check **www.PacktPub.com** for information on our titles